The Work of Christ

Bridges Youth Series

Kevin Stiffler,
Youth Editor

Mary Jaracz and
Virginia L. Wachenschwanz,
Layout and Design

Joseph D. Allison,
Publisher

Published quarterly for the teaching church by Warner Press, Inc., 1201 East Fifth Street, Anderson, Indiana 46012. Printed in the United States of America. For permissions and other editorial matters, contact: Coordinator of Publishing, PO Box 2420, Anderson, Indiana 46018-2420. Lessons based on International Sunday School lessons: the International Bible Lessons for Christian Teaching. Copyright © 1971 by Committee on Uniform Series. Scripture taken from the HOLY BIBLE, NEW INTERNATIONAL VERSION NIV®. Copyright © 1973, 1978, 1984 by International Bible Society. Used by permission of Zondervan Publishing House. All rights reserved.

ISBN-13: 978-1-59317-559-7

Warner Press
© Copyright by
Warner Press, Inc.

Contents

MW01204112

SESSION	TITLE

About this Book

The Case for Christ

If you grew up in church, your culture is influenced by Christ. For frequent churchgoers, the very flow of the week is shaped by the church: getting up early on Sundays for Sunday school and worship, eating out together or in someone's home, an afternoon of fun and relaxation, a return trip for evening worship (probably in clothes that were a little more casual than those worn in the morning), Mom or Dad gone to a board meeting on Tuesday night, and the fun of Wednesday night worship. Even if your family was very infrequent in church attendance, your life was still significantly influenced by Christ and the church: Easter and Christmas called for worship attendance, weddings and funerals were held in the church, school had an extended break around Christmastime (even if no one associated it with Christmas), and the pastor was called in times of extreme crisis.

The influence of Christ on North American culture can no longer be taken for granted. Public displays that include biblical themes and public use of prayer or most anything deemed to be "Christian" are banned with increasing frequency. The issue for many people is no longer how to get them into church, but how to help them even understand that there is a God. It is into this environment that God has called you to present the case for Christ. Your journey has intersected the journey of some teenagers—maybe a few of them, maybe a lot of them. Christ will draw them. You need to love them. Know why you believe what you believe. Get out of the box with your teaching methods. And watch God work!

Making the case,

Kevin Stiffler

Kevin Stiffler, Youth Editor of Bridges

Portable Sanctuary

The **Portable Sanctuary** is designed to be copied and distributed to students at the end of each week's session. This handout will continue the ideas from the session throughout the week with additional scripture references, stories, journaling, and prayer topics. This will give students an opportunity to establish some daily devotional time that builds on a consistent theme.

Encourage students to use the Portable Sanctuary, and lead them in this effort by using it yourself. Allow time at the beginning of each session to review last week's Portable Sanctuary and have some extra copies available for any students who were not present last week.

Digital Bridges is an interactive CD-ROM available for purchase to supplement this printed book.

From quarter to quarter Digital Bridges contains different things such as a video introduction to the book, teaching tips, videos, songs (that will also play with just a CD player), interactive games, projection sheets, color pictures and slide presentations, links to some great Web sites, and all of the printed curriculum in PDF format for you to customize and print at your convenience. These features can be used in preparation for and during your time in the classroom to enhance the teaching and learning experience.

Whenever you see (DB) in the book, it indicates a place where Digital Bridges can be used.

Authors

UNIT 1

Christ in Hebrews

Keah (Kendall) Redder is deciphering the ins and outs of married life as of June 2008. She and her husband Steve live in Colorado Springs, Colorado, where they spend their time drinking in the beauty and adventure that typifies the Rocky Mountains. Keah is addicted to coffee, Indie bookstores, and friends, particularly all at the same time. She is currently seeking the perfect job that involves students, ministry, music, and good pay — a chase after the wind? Perhaps. But, as Dickinson once said, "I dwell in possibility."

UNIT 2

Christ in the Gospels

The different sessions of Unit 2 were originally submitted by Doug Lucy, Jerry D. Lewis, Marty Samples, and Ann Simon, respectively. They were compiled, tweaked, massaged, and otherwise worked on by Kevin Stiffler. Kevin is a mechanical engineer and church volunteer in Tolare, California.

UNIT 3

Christ in Us

Sharon Bernhardt is a secondary school teacher. She also writes, edits, and translates for *Go! Magazine*, *World Harvest*, *Dreamlight*, and *Demand Studios*.

Bible Background was written by Merle D. Strege, professor of historical theology at Anderson University and Church of God historian.

Biblically Balanced

In what ways are we advised to be "balanced" in life? Eat a well-balanced diet. Maintain a well-balanced schedule. The word *balanced* can be loaded in some cases.

What does it mean to be *biblically* balanced? There are lots of ways to slice that one. How about equal amounts of Old and New Testament? That can be difficult to do, since there is lots more material in the Old than in the New. How about knowing the whole Bible? Starting at page 1 and reading through in order is not always the best approach.

This book is a part of the BRIDGES youth series, a series that seeks to cover every major teaching passage in the Bible every six years. That means that if you use each book in the series, you can cover all of the Scripture with your students in six years. No, this won't include every last word in the whole Bible, but you'll spend time in each book — and you'll give your students the whole picture. We'll "shake things up" a little, so that your class won't get bogged down by three months of Deuteronomy.

We often lament high schools that graduate students who can't read or add. The fault lies not with the students, but with the system that turned a blind eye to their need. If the youth group is graduating students who don't know which end of a Bible is up, well...what can we say? Some factors (such as student attitudes and attendance patterns) are out of our control. But the **scope** of what we teach, and the **sequence** in which we teach it, should be a slam dunk for us. BRIDGES can be a staple of your Sunday morning group, while you do topical things on Sunday nights or Wednesdays. Regardless of how the days of the week shake out, be sure to have a good plan!

CHRIST IN HEBREWS

The Book of Hebrews originally had some trouble being accepted into the New Testament canon. It was at first thought to be a letter of Paul; however, it has no signature, no personal greetings or salutation, or anything else to identify its authorship in this way. Its style and content are quite unique among all the books of the Bible. In many ways, Hebrews is a mystery! Yet in creative and beautiful ways it describes the mystery of Christ in ways that we can identify with and begin to understand.

Session 1 will look at the clear and powerful communication God brought through Jesus. Session 2 will examine Jesus' role as constant intercessor on our behalf. Session 3 will explore the salvation Christ offers to all who will accept it. Session 4 will deal with the loving discipline God gives to his children. Session 5 will study the security of a consistent, eternal Savior.

May you enjoy the mystery of Christ as God uses you to reveal it to your students.

Unit 1 Special Prep

SESSION 1—WARM UP, Option 2 (More Prep), calls for a ball of string and a pair of scissors. STARTING LINE, Option 1 (Younger Youth), requires modeling clay, paper, pens or pencils, and messages written out beforehand; you can also use the Digital BRIDGES CD, a computer, and a data projector. For FINISH LINE, Option 1 (Little Prep), you can use note cards. Option 2 (More Prep) calls for slips of paper with scripture assignments written on them.

SESSION 2—WARM UP, Option 2 (More Prep), requires a copy of the movie *The Wizard of Oz* and the necessary equipment to show it. FINISH LINE, Option 2 (More Prep), calls for small glass bottles and small slips of paper.

SESSION 3—WARM UP, Option 1 (Little Prep), requires calculators. Option 2 (More Prep) calls for the movie *Chariots of Fire* and the necessary equipment to show it. STARTING LINE, Option 1 (Younger Youth), requires newspaper or magazine ads, or Internet access. HOME STRETCH, Option 1 (Younger Youth), calls for a comfy chair and footstool. FINISH LINE, Option 2 (More Prep), requires a lab technician or other authority on blood to visit the class.

SESSION 4—For WARM UP, Option 1 (Little Prep), you can use copies of your youth group guidelines. Option 2 (More Prep) calls for two volleyballs or soccer balls and space for a relay race. HOME STRETCH, Option 1 (Younger Youth), requires tape. FINISH LINE, Option 2 (More Prep), calls for a creative place to discard things.

SESSION 5—For WARM UP, Option 2 (More Prep), you can use Monopoly money. STARTING LINE, Option 1 (Younger Youth), requires a "new" person to visit your class. HOME STRETCH, Option 1 (Younger Youth), calls for church leaders to visit the class. FINISH LINE, Option 2 (More Prep), requires small scraps of blanket-type cloth.

Leading into the Session

Warm Up

Option 1 Play two-minute intros.
LITTLE PREP

Option 2 Play the string game.
MORE PREP *Ball of string, pair of scissors*

Starting Line

Option 1 Communicate a message.
YOUNGER YOUTH *Modeling clay, paper, pens or pencils, messages written out beforehand; Digital* BRIDGES *CD, computer, and data projector (optional)*

Option 2 Learn ways God has communicated.
OLDER YOUTH *Bibles, Reproducible 1, pens or pencils*

Leading through the Session

Straight Away

Explore the Bible passage.
Bibles, Reproducible 2, pens or pencils

The Turn

Discuss God's new means to communicate.

Leading beyond the Session

Home Stretch

Option 1 Read a Bible story.
YOUNGER YOUTH *Bibles*

Option 2 Let God speak.
OLDER YOUTH *Bibles*

Finish Line

Option 1 Memorize a verse.
LITTLE PREP *Bibles; note cards, pens or pencils (optional)*

Option 2 Assign homework.
MORE PREP *Slips of paper with scripture assignments written on them*

SESSION 1

GETTING TO KNOW YOU

Bible Passage
Hebrews 1

Key Verse
In these last days he [God the Father] has spoken to us by his Son, whom he appointed heir of all things, and through whom he made the universe.
—Hebrews 1:2

Main Thought
God communicated through his Son Jesus.

Bible

Background

It once was believed that Paul wrote the discourse titled simply in New Testament Greek as "To the Hebrews." Today the consensus of scholarship is that we do not know the identity of the author. No signature appears, of course, and neither are there personal greetings or a salutation. This leads some scholars to conclude that Hebrews originally was a lengthy sermon or discourse rather than a letter. In any case, its subject matter and eloquence combine to give us some of the most memorable passages in all the New Testament.

Hebrews opens with a ringing affirmation of the supremacy of Christ over all created beings. What would necessitate such an endorsement? We must remember that the individual books of the New Testament were written at a moment when the Christian movement was still in the process of definition. Indeed, it is these books that shaped early Christianity against the efforts of those who interpreted Jesus very differently. Many early converts did not leave all of their religious assumptions behind when they joined what Acts calls simply "the Way." Thus some Gentile pagans retained ideas about the relationship of mind and body, while some Jewish Christians' firm belief in the one true God made it difficult for them to believe that Jesus Christ was fully divine. Hebrews reaffirms Christ's status as "the exact representation of [God's] being."

The debate over Christ's nature and relation to God the Father lasted into the fourth and fifth centuries. That it endured so long was partially due to several factors. The early church's doctrinal tradition was still developing. Christians did not agree on the twenty-seven books of the New Testament as canonical for at least two centuries after Christ; indeed, the canonical status of Hebrews was among the lengthiest disagreements. Early versions of the Apostle's Creed, a doctrinal summary that contained what Irenaeus, second-century bishop of Lyons and a vigorous heresy hunter, called the "rule of faith," were circulating. But church structure was not yet sufficiently established to enforce doctrinal uniformity.

In AD 325 the emperor Constantine convened a council of bishops at Nicea, a suburb of the new imperial city of Constantinople. Some twelve years earlier Constantine had legalized Christianity and had only recently succeeded in politically reunifying the Roman Empire. He was not about to watch a bitter theological dispute tear apart the empire he had worked so hard to unify. The assembled church leaders produced the Nicene Creed, one of the most enduring statements of Trinitarian Christian doctrine, including its affirmation that Christ is of the same essence as God the Father. The creed did not eliminate all variant opinions of the nature of Christ, but it was a major milestone in a debate that stretched all the way back to Hebrews.

OPTION 1 (LITTLE PREP)

Play two-minute intros.

Ask the students to divide into pairs. If you can, facilitate the pairing so that students are with someone they do not know well. Instruct the pairs that they will have two minutes to find out five facts about each other that no one else in the room knows. These facts can be as silly or serious as the students would like. After the two minutes is passed, invite each student to introduce his or her partner to the rest of the group. Then discuss the following questions:

Warm Up

- **What were some results of this activity?** Ultimately, the purpose was for each student to get to know his or her partner better.
- **How were these results achieved?** Each student got to know his or her partner through communication.
- **Why do you think communication is so important?** It is a means for us to know others and to be known by them.

Say, **Communication with God is a way we can get to know him.**

* *

OPTION 2 (MORE PREP)

Play the string game.

Pass around a ball of string and scissors and ask each student to cut off a piece. Give no instructions as to the appropriate length of string to cut. Then ask the students to divide into pairs, taking their strings with them. If you can, facilitate the pairing so that students are with someone they do not know well. Once in pairs, provide the students time to share facts about themselves, with these guidelines:

> *Note:*
>
> If you sent the Portable Sanctuary home with students last week, take some time at the beginning of this session to review and discuss their experience.

1. The students must share facts that no one else in the room will know.
2. The students must share one fact for every inch of string they cut.

Allow enough time (within reason, if someone cut a very long piece of string) for students to share their required number of facts. Then ask each student to introduce his or her partner to the rest of the group. After every student has shared, discuss the following questions:

- **What were some results of this activity?** The students may share many fun lessons relating to the length of string, but ultimately, the purpose was for each student to get to know his or her partner better. The string was just a means to an end.
- **How were these results achieved?** Each student got to know his or her partner through communication.
- **Why do you think communication is so important?** It is a means for us to know others and to be known by them.

Say, **Communication with God is a way we can get to know him.**

James B.
1. I like Italian food
2. I would like to travel the world
3. I have the best wife & kids ever
4. Had a brother that drowned
5. Have a Duck as a brother

Starting Line

OPTION 1 (YOUNGER YOUTH)

Communicate a message.

Separate your students into groups of two or three. You will need at least four groups; depending on your number of students, you may modify the activity. Assign to each group a message and a means of communication. Be sure that each group keeps its assignment secret from the rest of the students. The goal is for each group to communicate its message to the rest of the students through the means assigned. However, if the students are using a verbal means of communication, they may not say or sing any of the actual words in the message (in other words, they must communicate the words of the message by using other words). Following are some examples of messages and means, to be used in any combination. Feel free to modify as necessary to fit your group dynamics:

Message
The building is on fire.
I can't wait for Christmas.
I would like a pizza.
It is slightly cloudy with a chance of rain.

Means
Singing
Gesturing or acting
Clay modeling
Drawing

After each group has communicated its message, discuss the following questions:

- **What was fun about this activity?**
- **What was difficult about this activity?**
- **What are some other forms of communication people have used over the years?** Some examples include smoke signals, drumming, public speaking, writing, telegraph, radio, telephone, movies, television, e-mail, texting, blogging, social networking sites, and so forth. If you have access to the Digital BRIDGES CD, a computer, and a data projector, show the "Communication" video. Even though most of your students won't understand what was said (Isaiah 42:1 was quoted), sign language is a valid form of communication for those who understand it.
- **What are some forms of communication that God used in the Bible?** This is not meant to be an exhaustive list, only some examples of ways God has communicated with his people. You may need to be prepared to explain the bare bones of some major stories mentioned here. God spoke directly to Adam and Eve (Genesis 1:28). He spoke to Abram through a vision (Genesis 15:1). He spoke to Moses out of a burning bush (Exodus 3:4). He spoke to Elijah in a still small voice (1 Kings 19:11–13). He spoke through prophets such as Jeremiah (Jeremiah 1:9–10). He spoke to Joseph through a dream (Matthew 2:13). He sent an angel to speak to Mary (Luke 1:26–33).

When you are ready to move on, say, **Let's take a look at Jesus to see how he was an entirely new form of communication.**

OPTION 2 (OLDER YOUTH)

Learn ways God has communicated.

Explain that in the Bible, God used many different forms of communication when speaking with his people. In this activity, you will discover some of those forms as they are described in the Bible.

Distribute copies of "Can You Hear Me Now?" (Reproducible 1) along with pens or pencils. You may choose to split up the verses in whatever way works best for your group. Allow time for the students to read their assigned verses and make notes: **To whom is God speaking? Through what means?** Then ask the students to share what they have discovered with the rest of the group. You may choose to write the students' discoveries on the board:

- *Genesis 1:28–31—Direct speech*
  God spoke with Adam and Eve from the moment of their creation, giving them the charge to be fruitful and take care of the Earth.
- *Genesis 15:1–6—Visions*
  God came to Abram in a vision, telling him not to be afraid. In the vision, God showed Abram the night sky and told him his offspring would be as numerous as the stars.
- *Genesis 16:7–10—Angels*
  An angel from the Lord appeared to Hagar, Sarai's servant, and told her that God would give her many descendants. You may choose to explain that God did indeed give Hagar many children through her son Ishmael, also a son of Abram (Abraham).
- *Genesis 20:1–7—Dreams*
  Abraham lied about his marriage to Sarah; so Abimelech, King of Gerar, took her as his wife. But God saved Sarah by going to Abimelech in a dream and revealing the true relationship between Sarah and Abraham.
- *Exodus 3:1–6—Burning bush*
  God got Moses' attention by appearing in a burning bush in the desert. Out of the bush, he spoke and called Moses to deliver his people from Pharaoh's oppression.
- *1 Kings 19:11–13—A whisper*
  God called Elijah to wait for him to come. The Lord was not in the great wind, the earthquake, or a fire; he came in a gentle whisper. This is where we get the idea that God often speaks in a "still, small voice."
- *Jeremiah 1:9–10, 2:1–3—Prophets*
  The Lord put his words in the mouth of the prophet Jeremiah so that he would be the voice of God to the people of Israel. The Lord told Jeremiah what to say every step of the way.
- *Daniel 5:1–6, 25–28—Writing on the wall*
  King Belshazzar was quite conceited and did not humble himself before the Lord, so God sent a hand that wrote a mysterious message. Daniel interpreted the message as the king's own death sentence.

When you are ready to move on, say, **Let's take a look at Jesus to see how he was an entirely new form of communication.**

11

Straight Away

Explore the Bible passage.

Read together Hebrews 1. You may wish to break up the reading into smaller sections. Discuss the following questions:

- **What is the main point of this chapter, and why do you think it was important when this was written?** Jesus is superior to all things, including angels. In the early church, some people were not certain just how to define Jesus. Was he human? Was he God? The writer of Hebrews gave a good explanation of the supremacy of Christ.
- **Before Jesus, how did God speak to humankind?** God spoke at various times and in various ways. Help the students make the connection between this and the previous activities in this session, discovering some of these means of communication.
- **How does Jesus speak to us for God?** The Gospels give us a record of many of Jesus' words while he was here on Earth. Point out that the things Jesus did—his dying on the cross, his healings, and his compassion—also speak to us of God's love.
- **What are some specific descriptors of Jesus given in this chapter?** For younger youth, focus on verses 2 and 3: Jesus is heir of (the one who will inherit) all things; he helped form the universe; he radiates God's glory; he is the exact representation of God, he provided purification for sins. For older youth, distribute copies of "Who Do You Say I Am?" (Reproducible 2). As per the instructions, students should find each of the seven descriptive phrases in verses 2 and 3 and put them in their own words (they can do this alone, in groups, or all together). Some possibilities:

  1. **Jesus is appointed heir of all things.** Jesus will receive everything in this world that is God's.
  2. **God made the universe through Jesus.** Jesus was there in the beginning, with God before and in Creation.
  3. **Jesus is the radiance of God's glory.** Just as one cannot separate the sun's rays from the sun itself, so Jesus cannot be separated from God. They are one and the same.
  4. **Jesus is the representation of God's being.** Jesus is not just a reflection of God. He *is* God.
  5. **Jesus sustains all things through his powerful word.** All of creation, including each of us, relies upon Jesus for life and meaning.
  6. **Jesus provided purification from sin.** He did this through his death on the cross.
  7. **Jesus sat down at the right hand of God in heaven.** The act of sitting down means that the task of forgiving sin, mentioned above, is complete once and for all.

- **The writer gave a lot of quotes in this chapter. Who was being quoted, and whom was this person talking about?** God was being quoted, from the Old Testament (the students' Bibles should have scripture references for each quote). God was speaking about Jesus.

- **From these verses, how did (does) God treat Jesus?** God is Father to Jesus; he set Jesus above everyone and everything else eternally and set him apart through the act of anointing him.
- **Why would the author need to distinguish Jesus from angels?** Explain that one of the things the New Testament church did was begin to nail down some accurate descriptions of Jesus. (Remember, there had never been anyone like him before! We almost take his identity as God's Son for granted, but that belief was not as established then.) Jesus did miracles (some of which defied the laws of physics), and at times after his resurrection he appeared and disappeared at will. Jesus also said that he was from God. Many people may have thought that Jesus was just a special kind of angel.
- **What does this chapter say about Jesus' place in time?** He was there from the beginning, and he will be around forever. Jesus remains. No matter what is going on around us, we can trust that Jesus will be the same and will be there for us.

Say, **Jesus' eternal nature and link with God make him a great way for God to communicate with us.**

The Turn

Discuss God's new means to communicate.

Help your students understand more about Jesus as God's communicator by discussing the following questions:

- **Why is it important that God spoke in a new way through Jesus?** Ask students to recall again the WARM UP activity from today. We communicate with others so we can get to know them. By communicating through Jesus, God provided a totally new and powerful way for us to get to know him.
- **Why communicate through Jesus? Why not just talk to us directly, write it down, or something else?** In the early days of Creation, God often spoke directly with human beings—and they still messed things up. God spoke and still speaks to us through his words in the Bible. In Christ, God became one of us. This makes a close, intimate relationship with the Father possible.
- **Does God still communicate in ways other than through Jesus?** God's Word is still valid, and God still speaks to our hearts through the Holy Spirit—but Jesus is the One to whom the Bible points, and the standard by which we understand all other communication from God.

Say, **As God's Son, Jesus is God on Earth—we can learn a lot about God by studying Jesus.**

Home Stretch

OPTION 1 (YOUNGER YOUTH)

Read a Bible story.

Help your students understand some of what is communicated from God through Jesus by reading together Matthew 19:13–15 and discussing the following questions:

- **Why did people bring children to Jesus?** They wanted Jesus to pray for the children.
- **Why do you think the disciples rebuked, or scolded, the people?** Maybe they thought Jesus, an important man, did not have time for little children.
- **How did Jesus respond?** Jesus not only prayed for them as the people asked, but he also said that something as great as the kingdom of heaven belonged to people as seemingly insignificant as children.
- **What can we learn about God from this passage?** Here are some possibilities:

  - God wants to give us good things.
  - Sometimes we may not understand how God thinks, and we may try to do the very opposite of what God wants.
  - God loves each of us, but beyond that, he loves the seemingly insignificant parts of us.
  - In God's kingdom, even the smallest are great.

When you are ready to move on, say, **When you look at the life of Jesus, watching what he did and reading what he said, you have the chance to hear and understand God the Father.**

· ·

OPTION 2 (OLDER YOUTH)

Let God speak.

Help your students understand some of what is communicated from God through Jesus by reading together Matthew 14:13–21. Ask, **What can we learn about God from studying this passage about Jesus?** Push your students to go deep with this passage. Here are some things that might be noted:

- Just prior to this, Jesus received word that his relative John the Baptist was beheaded by King Herod. His response seems to be what many of us might do—he went to be alone.
- Even though he was likely in a state of grief, Jesus had compassion on the crowds, spending time with them and healing them.
- Jesus first asked the disciples to solve the problem. When they could not, Jesus blessed the meal. However, instead of handing it out himself, Jesus let the disciples distribute the meal. Perhaps this was not just a practical decision, but also a good chance for the disciples to experience the miracle and the ministry up close.

- This story speaks to us of God's heart, his compassion, and his desire to involve us in the work of his kingdom.

When you are ready to move on, say, **When you look at the life of Jesus, watching what he did and reading what he said, you have the chance to hear and understand God the Father.**

Option 1 (Little Prep)

Memorize a verse.

As a reminder of the message from this session, help your students to memorize the following verse from the New Living Translation:

"Christ is the visible image of the invisible God" (Colossians 1:15).

If you choose, you can encourage the students to write the verse down on a note card so they can post it in a visible location, in order to remind them that just as Christ is the image of God, we are living images of Christ.

Close the session with a prayer similar to the following:

Father God, we thank you for sending your Son as a new way to communicate with us. Help us learn that as we grow closer to Jesus, we grow closer to you. In his name we pray, Amen.

Finish Line

• •

Option 2 (More Prep)

Assign homework.

Write the following scripture passages on slips of paper; make duplicates so that there are enough slips for each student to have one:

Mark 11:15–19
Matthew 8:1–4
Luke 10:38–42
John 21:15–19
Luke 19:1–10

Pass out the slips of paper and explain that each scripture is a story about Jesus. Over the next week, each student should read the story assigned and bring back some ideas about what we can learn about God through the story. (***Note:*** What the students do not know is that these scripture assignments follow along with this session's Portable Sanctuary, so be sure the Portable goes home with them as well.) At the beginning of the next session, be sure to ask the students their thoughts on the scriptures.

Close the session with a prayer similar to the following:

Father God, we thank you for sending your Son as a new way to communicate with us. Help us learn that as we grow closer to Jesus, we grow closer to you. In his name we pray, Amen.

> *Note:*
>
> Don't forget to distribute copies of the Portable Sanctuary to students before they go.

Can You Hear Me Now?

Read the passages listed below and distinguish the means God used in each to communicate. Make further notes about the message and situation.

Genesis 1:28–31
Means: _Direct Speech_
Situation: _____

Genesis 15:1–6
Means: _____
Situation: _____

Genesis 16:7–10
Means: _____
Situation: _____

Genesis 20:1–7
Means: _____
Situation: _____

Exodus 3:1–6
Means: _____
Situation: _____

1 Kings 19:11–13
Means: _____
Situation: _____

Jeremiah 1:9–10; 2:1–3
Means: _____
Situation: _____

Daniel 5:1–6, 25–28
Means: _____
Situation: _____

Who Do You Say I Am?

In Hebrews 1:2–3, there are seven descriptive phrases about Jesus.
Find each phrase and put it in your own words:

ORIGINAL PHRASE   **IN YOUR OWN WORDS....**

1. _____   _____
   _____   _____
   _____   _____

2. _____   _____
   _____   _____
   _____   _____

3. _____   _____
   _____   _____
   _____   _____

4. _____   _____
   _____   _____
   _____   _____

5. _____   _____
   _____   _____
   _____   _____

6. _____   _____
   _____   _____
   _____   _____

7. _____   _____
   _____   _____
   _____   _____

Portable Sanctuary

Day 1

The Right Kind of Anger

For centuries, Jews came to the temple in Jerusalem to offer animal sacrifices for their sins. Ever since the time of Moses, this is what God had required of his people. But by the time Jesus came on the scene, sacrificing had become more of a business than a true spiritual practice. The temple was a marketplace for buying and selling sacrificial animals. It's no wonder that when Jesus saw this, he got truly angry and drove the merchants out of the temple. They had turned worship into a business transaction instead of an act from the heart.

Questions and Suggestions

• What is the difference between a right kind of anger and a wrong kind of anger?

• How did Jesus display a right kind of anger?

• What does this Jesus story reveal to us about God the Father?

• Read Mark 11:15–19 for the story of Jesus' anger in the temple.

• Take stock of your tendency for anger—do you get angry about the right things, or do you tend to get angry about things that ultimately do not matter? Pray about it.

Day 2

The Untouchables

Leprosy is a nasty skin disease that ultimately causes one's body to literally fall apart. It's also seriously contagious. Even today, people with leprosy are generally quarantined and avoided. But in Jesus' time, without the medical help we enjoy today, the problem was rampant. These people were the outcasts of society, not even allowed to live

Questions and Suggestions

• Does this story bother you at all? Why or why not?

• What does this Jesus story reveal to us about God the Father?

• Read Luke 19:1–10 for the story about Jesus calling Zacchaeus out.

• Identify the "Zacs" in your life—how can you treat them the way Jesus did?

N O T E S

within the city walls. Jesus healed a man with leprosy—a truly radical act. Not only did he get close to the man, he actually touched him. Jesus did not care about his own skin, only that he could heal this man—a complete outcast and social misfit.

Questions and Suggestions

- What was radical about Jesus' healing of a man with leprosy?
- How do you respond to the "lepers" in your own life?
- What does this Jesus story reveal to us about God the Father?
- Read Matthew 8:1–4 for the story of Jesus healing a man with leprosy.
- This week, go out of your way to come in contact with an outcast in your world.

Day 3
Busy Body

Jesus was a good friend with sisters Mary and Martha. On one particular visit, Martha was consumed with preparing her house and a meal, while her sister Mary was simply sitting with Jesus and not lifting a finger to help. Martha tried to get Mary to help, but Jesus rebuked her, saying that Mary chose what was better. Could it be true that Jesus valued time spent with a dear friend over the hustle and bustle of preparation and presentation?

Questions and Suggestions

- What does this story say about our culture's tendency toward busy-ness?
- Take stock of your life. Are you more Mary or Martha?
- What does this Jesus story reveal to us about God the Father?
- Read Luke 10:38–42 for the story about Jesus and the two sisters.
- Spend time this week sitting at the Lord's feet. Instead of being busy for God, just be with God.

Day 4
Third Time's a Charm

On the night Jesus was arrested, Peter denied three times even knowing Jesus. Peter—one of Jesus' closest followers. Peter—who said he would follow Jesus anywhere. So it's no surprise that after Jesus' resurrection, he offered Peter a chance to redeem himself. Jesus asked Peter three times if he loved him, matching the number of times Peter had denied Jesus. Jesus cared enough to forgive and offer a second chance, and Peter ended up being the leader of the first group of Christ-followers, later known as Christians.

Questions and Suggestions

- Do you ever struggle with thinking that God might not forgive what you have done?
- How has God already offered you second chances?
- What does this Jesus story reveal to us about God the Father?
- Read John 21:15–19 for the story about Jesus returning Peter to right relationship with him.
- Pray that God will help you accept the forgiveness he already offers.

Day 5
Dinner Guest

In Jesus' time, tax collectors were like the scum of the earth. They made their money by overcharging on Roman taxes, and they usually sported a cushy lifestyle as proof. You might think that Jesus would condemn such a man as a sinner, but in fact he did the opposite. While walking through Jerusalem, Jesus spotted Zacchaeus, a well-known tax collector, and invited himself over to dinner at Zac's house. Jesus did not hold Zac's lifestyle against him; he simply accepted him and offered him the same promise of love and acceptance as he might any other person.

Leading into the Session

Warm Up

Option 1 Practice intercession.
LITTLE PREP

Option 2 View a movie clip.
MORE PREP
A copy of The Wizard of Oz *and the necessary equipment to show it*

Starting Line

Option 1 Share "approaching" stories.
YOUNGER YOUTH

Option 2 Discuss God's approachability.
OLDER YOUTH

Leading through the Session

Straight Away

Explore the Bible passages.
Bibles, Reproducible 1

The Turn

Discuss our need for intercession.

Leading beyond the Session

Home Stretch

Option 1 Discuss angels.
YOUNGER YOUTH *Bibles, Reproducible 2*

Option 2 Share an intercession story.
OLDER YOUTH

Finish Line

Option 1 Intercede for one another.
LITTLE PREP

Option 2 Make a message in a bottle.
MORE PREP
Small glass bottles, small slips of paper, pens or pencils, chalkboard or dry erase board

---

SESSION 2

A FRIEND IN HIGH PLACES

Bible Passages
Hebrews 7:1–3, 11–28

Key Verse
He [Christ] is able to save completely those who come to God through him, because he always lives to intercede for them.
—Hebrews 7:25

Main Thought
Jesus' constant intercession enables him to be a constant help to us.

Bible Background

Most ordained Protestant clergy are called *ministers* in distinction from Roman Catholic priests. One of the Latin words for priest is *pontifex*, which comes from the same root as the word for bridge. In a general religious sense this metaphor captures the essence of the idea of priesthood; priests link people with the god they worship, as bridges link two sides of a river or chasm. The word *minister*, on the other hand, connotes service, as in, "Our pastor ministered to us in our time of need." Priests serve a particularly distinctive role in worship, where traditionally they have been understood to represent the people before God. This distinctive role separates clergy and laity; some rites are reserved exclusively to priests. For example, in Catholicism only ordained priests may officiate at the service of the Mass, the Lord's Supper. A similar separation exists among some Protestant denominations, especially those with a strong sense of tradition. The idea of the special nature and functions of priesthood runs all the way back to ancient times, when priests conducted sacrifices for the people.

The Roman destruction of the temple and Jerusalem in AD 70 effectively ended the Jewish priesthood, but the emergence of rabbis had already modified the office. A rabbi was, and remains, fundamentally a teacher. So, for example, Ezra was a man learned in the Law of Moses who taught that Law to the people. The office of rabbi began to develop during the Babylonian exile, when many Israelites were far from home and those in Jerusalem could not offer sacrifices at a temple that lay in ruins. The temple was eventually rebuilt and the sacrificial system and priesthood restored, but the ensuing years brought another new development in Jewish life—the synagogue. In contrast to the temple, a place of sacrifice, synagogues were places of religious teaching as well as centers of community life. Rabbis were more likely to function at schools and synagogues than at the temple. In the three years of his public ministry Jesus was frequently called a rabbi, but nobody would have thought of him as a priest, let alone the high priest.

Hebrews uses the office of priest to emphasize the exalted status of Jesus Christ, a basic theme of this discourse. Jesus is the great high priest. He no longer makes sacrifice for sins; his sacrifice on Calvary was "once for all" (7:27). Furthermore, unlike mortal high priests who die and who must offer sacrifice for their own sins as well as the sins of others, Jesus is eternally the high priest and himself without sin. As all priests, Jesus the great high priest intercedes for us with God, but Christ "is able to save completely those who come to God through him, because he always lives...." (7:25).

OPTION 1 (LITTLE PREP)

Practice intercession.

Conduct some kind of a contest where one student tries to take something from another student or come in contact with another student. For example, you could hand one student a book or some other object and challenge another student to try to take that object, or challenge one student to try tagging another student on the head. Ask for three volunteers: one to try to touch/take something, one to try to avoid being touched or having something taken, and one to come between the two to help the second avoid being touched or "robbed." (Be sure to consider how your students deal with rough activities, and be careful not to let any people or objects get hurt.)

After your little contest, ask, **What was the "middle" person doing?** He or she was trying to help someone by coming between that person and the attacker. Explain that this is one form of intercession. To intercede means to come between someone and another person or thing on behalf of that person.

Say, **We have all interceded—and been interceded for—at one time or another.**

Warm Up

> *Note:*
> If you sent the Portable Sanctuary home with students last week, take some time at the beginning of this session to review and discuss their experience.

OPTION 2 (MORE PREP)

View a movie clip.

Show the students a clip from *The Wizard of Oz* in order to help them start thinking about approaching God. To set the clip up, say something similar to the following:

Many of you likely know the story of *The Wizard of Oz*. Dorothy, a girl from Kansas, finds herself in the strange land of Oz. Together with her friends the Scarecrow, the Tin Man, and the Cowardly Lion, Dorothy goes to the Emerald City for an audience with the Wizard of Oz, where they will each ask for what they need. In this scene, Dorothy and her friends first meet the Wizard of Oz.

Play scene 39, "Meeting the Wizard of Oz." Start at approximately 1:08:00, when the four friends are walking in to see the Wizard. Stop at approximately 1:12:00, after the lion jumps out the window.

Following the clip, discuss the following questions:

- **Why do you think the four friends were so scared?** Ultimately, they were scared because of the Wizard's fierce reputation.
- **How do you think the Wizard's chamber contributed to their fear?**
- **What parallels do you see between the way the four friends approached the Wizard and the way people sometimes approach God?** Some people approach God with fear and trembling, afraid of God's wrath.
- **Do you think this attitude is a good one to have? Why or why not?**

Say, **Some people are easier to approach than others.**

OPTION 1 (YOUNGER YOUTH)

Share "approaching" stories.

Invite students to share about times when they have been very fearful to approach someone else. Perhaps one student set the kitchen on fire and was terrified for his father to come home; perhaps another student got in trouble at school and was afraid to have to go see the strict principal. Be sure to share an "approaching" story of your own. Point out that we are afraid to approach some people because they have a reputation for being strict or mean. Referring back to the stories your students told, ask, **After you approached the person, were things as bad as you thought they would be?** Invite students to respond.

When you are ready to move on, say, **Let's learn a little bit about approaching God.**

OPTION 2 (OLDER YOUTH)

Discuss God's approachability.

Discuss the following questions:

- **What do you think are some common ways people think about or envision God?** Some answers might include these ways: as an old grandfather figure, as a mean cop ready to pull someone over, as an uninterested scientist, and so forth.
- **Where do you think people get these notions about God?** Our images of God are usually based on the characteristics we think he has: wise = old or a scientist; strict = a cop; and so forth.
- **Do you think God is pretty approachable or mostly unapproachable? Why?** If your students are comfortable, invite them to share personal stories about how they feel about approaching God.

Say, **Let's see how we know we can approach God with confidence.**

Explore the Bible passages.

Before you read today's Bible passage, ask, **What is the purpose of a priest?** Help your students understand that in a strict sense, a priest stands between the people and God in a bridge role. A priest performs duties on behalf of the people in God's presence.

Distribute to students copies of "Approaching God" (Reproducible 1) or show it as a projection. This handout reproduces the text of Hebrews 7:1–3, 11–28 in the New Living Translation. (Today's passages are somewhat confusing in the NIV.) Invite a student to read aloud Hebrews 7:1–3, 11–19. Then discuss the following questions:

- **Who was this Melchizedek mentioned here?** He was a king and a priest. Abraham recognized him as a very high priest and tithed to him a tenth of everything he owned. Nothing is known about Melchizedek's genealogy, so he was somewhat of a mysterious legend. Melchizedek lived before there was a set standard for the Israelite priesthood; eventually it was set up so that only members of the tribe of Levi were priests. Melchizedek was not a Levite—he lived before Levi was born.
- **How is Jesus similar to Melchizedek?** Like Melchizedek, Jesus was not from the tribe of Levi (he was from the tribe of Judah). They were priests of a different class entirely—so "high" that they didn't have to be Levites.

Invite another student to read aloud Hebrews 7:20–25. Then discuss the following questions:

- **How is it that Jesus was made a priest?** God took an oath that sealed Jesus' priesthood. This was God's intent for Jesus, that he be made a "bridge" between God and humankind.
- **Why will Jesus' priesthood never end?** Jesus was raised from the dead, and he still lives. Traditional priests served until they died, but Jesus will never die.
- **Why is Jesus' eternal priesthood exciting news for us?** Jesus' priesthood continues forever, so he is always able to perform the priestly duty of approaching God for us. We never need to be afraid to approach God because Jesus is always there with us, speaking and praying on our behalf.

Invite another student to read aloud Hebrews 7:26–28. Then discuss the following questions:

- **How is Jesus different from the other high priests?** He is eternal. Regular priests sacrificed repeatedly for the people's sins and for their own sins. When Jesus died on the cross, he himself was a blameless (without sin) sacrifice. He took care of the issue forever.
- **Why is this important for us?** Jesus' sacrifice on the cross forever removed our need to sacrifice for our own sins. As our high priest, Jesus offered the ultimate sacrifice; therefore, he removed the barrier between us and God.

Say, **Jesus lives forever, as intercessor in the presence of God.**

Discuss our need for intercession.

Invite your students to think back to times when they could have used an intercessor. If you used STARTING LINE, Option 1 (Younger Youth), refer to the stories your students shared. Ask, **Could you have used an intercessor? How would that have helped?** An intercessor is like a defender, someone who is on our side and who comes between us and the consequences we might have received. If a bully is threatening us on the schoolyard, an intercessor would intercede for us (come between us and the bully). If our parents are upset with us over something, an intercessor would intercede on our behalf with our parents. And if we have any sort of trouble in life, Christ lives to intercede for us—to take our needs to God, who can take care of them.

Say, **Jesus' constant intercession enables him to be a constant help to us.**

The Turn

Home Stretch

OPTION 1 (YOUNGER YOUTH)

Discuss angels.

Distribute copies of "Angels Aware" (Reproducible 2) and spend some time discussing angels with your students. What do they believe about angels? What do they know about angels? How could what we know of angels perhaps cause some people to think that Jesus was an angel? Point out that there are many things we just don't know about angels. We do know that the appearance of angels in the Bible is almost always associated with praising God, with miraculous events, and with the deliverance of news about the work of God. (The term *angel* can also be translated as "messenger.")

When you are ready to move on, say, **Jesus did many things that angels do—but he does much, much more.**

. . . .

OPTION 2 (OLDER YOUTH)

Share an intercession story.

Share the following true intercession story with your students (it is also available on the Digital BRIDGES CD as a projection):

George Nakajima taught at Asbury Theological Seminary in the 1970s. Here's how he was healed of an intestinal disorder, which had required several surgeries in Japan and the United States:

My healing is due to the prayers of many friends, both known and unknown. Of course, God used brilliant doctors, excellent hospital equipment, and high-developed medical science. But there are many things about my healing that cannot be explained, even by the doctors. My doctor told one of my friends that my case was a miracle.

…The idea of a special healing service was suggested to me by my pastor, Rev. Clyde Van Valin. He helped to prepare me for the healing service.

Within a short time, three men of God—my pastor; Mr. John Fitch, a dedicated layman; and the president of the Seminary—came to my hospital room for the healing service. They anointed me, laid hands on me, and prayed for my healing.

During the healing service, the president of the Seminary reminded me… that faith must have some imagination in it. He said, "Imagine yourself healed by God and for the glory of God." I immediately imagined myself healed by God and back in Japan witnessing to my own people.

I want to testify that from the time of the healing service in my hospital room, I began to recover. I amazed the doctors. There was no fourth operation. My meals were increased little by little. My body began to function more normally.

I returned to my home…I have been healed by the mercy and power of God.

Discuss this story with your students. Do they know anyone who has had such a "divine healing" experience? Point out that this story shows the power of intercession—people going before God on behalf of a man's desperate need.

When you are ready to move on, say, **Jesus intercedes before God for our needs every day.**

> *Note:*
>
> See Frank Bateman Stanger, *God's Healing Community* (Nappanee, Ind.: Evangel Publishing House, 2000) 83, 84.

OPTION 1 (LITTLE PREP)

Finish Line

Intercede for one another.

Explain that in Jesus we have a high priest who prays for us, making it easy for us to approach God. As followers of Christ, we are called to follow his example. We, too, can go to God on one another's behalf.

Invite your students to break up into pairs and allow them time to share prayer requests and pray for one another. After ample time for partner prayer, close the session with a communal prayer similar to the following:

Father God, we thank you that your Son Jesus comes to you on our behalf. May we learn to come boldly and fearlessly to you in behalf of others. In Jesus' name we pray, Amen.

• •

OPTION 2 (MORE PREP)

> *Note:*
>
> Don't forget to distribute copies of the Portable Sanctuary to students before they go.

Make a message in a bottle.

Explain that because we know Jesus is our high priest, praying on our behalf, we can come into God's presence without fear. No longer do we have to send our prayers to God like messages in a bottle, not knowing if God will truly hear us. Jesus makes sure that he does. Your students will be taking home a small reminder of this fact by each making a message in a bottle.

Bring to class small glass bottles, enough for each student to have one. You can find such bottles at a dollar store or the like. If you have problems finding bottles, you could even use small bud vases. Give a bottle to each student, and distribute slips of paper along with pens or pencils. Write the following on the board:

Because of Christ and our faith in him, we can now come boldly and confidently into God's presence (Ephesians 3:12, NLT).

Invite the students to write the verse on their slips of paper and put them in the bottle as reminders that they do have assurance of coming into God's presence without fear.

Close with a prayer similar to the following:

Father God, we thank you that your Son Jesus comes to you on our behalf. May we learn to come boldly and fearlessly to you through your Son. In Jesus' name we pray, Amen.

"I don't think you have held my hand once since
you became the treasurer of the youth group!"

Approaching God

Hebrews 7:1–3 (NLT)

This Melchizedek was king of the city of Salem and also a priest of God Most High. When Abraham was returning home after winning a great battle against the kings, Melchizedek met him and blessed him. Then Abraham took a tenth of all he had captured in battle and gave it to Melchizedek. The name Melchizedek means "king of justice," and king of Salem means "king of peace." There is no record of his father or mother or any of his ancestors—no beginning or end to his life. He remains a priest forever, resembling the Son of God.

Hebrews 7:11–19

So if the priesthood of Levi, on which the law was based, could have achieved the perfection God intended, why did God need to establish a different priesthood, with a priest in the order of Melchizedek instead of the order of Levi and Aaron?

And if the priesthood is changed, the law must also be changed to permit it. For the priest we are talking about belongs to a different tribe, whose members have never served at the altar as priests. What I mean is, our Lord came from the tribe of Judah, and Moses never mentioned priests coming from that tribe.

This change has been made very clear since a different priest, who is like Melchizedek, has appeared. Jesus became a priest, not by meeting the physical requirement of belonging to the tribe of Levi, but by the power of a life that cannot be destroyed. And the psalmist pointed this out when he prophesied,

"You are a priest forever in the order of Melchizedek."

Yes, the old requirement about the priesthood was set aside because it was weak and useless. For the law never made anything perfect. But now we have confidence in a better hope, through which we draw near to God.

Hebrews 7:20–28

This new system was established with a solemn oath. Aaron's descendants became priests without such an oath, but there was an oath regarding Jesus. For God said to him,

"The Lord has taken an oath and will not break his vow:
   'You are a priest forever.'"

Because of this oath, Jesus is the one who guarantees this better covenant with God.

There were many priests under the old system, for death prevented them from remaining in office. But because Jesus lives forever, his priesthood lasts forever. Therefore he is able, once and forever, to save those who come to God through him. He lives forever to intercede with God on their behalf.

He is the kind of high priest we need because he is holy and blameless, unstained by sin. He has been set apart from sinners and has been given the highest place of honor in heaven. Unlike those other high priests, he does not need to offer sacrifices every day. They did this for their own sins first and then for the sins of the people. But Jesus did this once for all when he offered himself as the sacrifice for the people's sins. The law appointed high priests who were limited by human weakness. But after the law was given, God appointed his Son with an oath, and his Son has been made the perfect High Priest forever.

Angels Aware

Angels rejoice when a sinner repents (see Luke 15:10).

Angels are often invisible to human eyes (see 2 Kings 6:15–17).

Angels are "ministering spirits," serving humankind (see Hebrews 1:14).

Angels are mentioned throughout the Bible, all the way from Genesis (3:24) to Revelation (22:6).

Angels have appeared in visions (see Matthew 1:20).

The type of angels known as seraphs are described as having wings (see Isaiah 6:2)—but most descriptions of angels in the Bible do not mention any wings.

Angels are immortal (see Luke 20:34–36).

Angels have appeared in bodily form (see Acts 12:6–10).

Two angels are mentioned by name in the Bible: Michael (see Revelation 12:7) and Gabriel (see Luke 1:19).

Portable Sanctuary

NOTES

Day 1

The Tithe

Some people are amazed at how a tithe (giving 10 percent of what you make to God) could possibly work in their lives. *I'm barely getting by as it is! How can I give God ten dollars of every hundred I make?* Yet multitudes of people who have tithed faithfully for years will testify that God takes great care of them. They do better financially when they honor God with 10 percent than when they keep it all for themselves. Abraham gave the first recorded tithe—and his life was truly blessed by God.

Questions and Suggestions

- Read Hebrews 7:1–3. What do you think caused Abraham to tithe?
- Do you tithe? Even if your income is small or sporadic, give tithing a try and see what God will do.

Day 2

Job Selection

What if you were required to select the same career your mom or dad had? If your parents own their own business and you enjoy that business, this might not be such a bad thing. I had a friend in high school whose dad owned a tire shop. My friend has worked at that tire shop since he was a kid. He enjoys the business. Someday he will own that tire shop. The Levites were expected to enter the "family business" of being a priest. They really didn't have much choice in the matter.

- Read Hebrews 7:11–17. What do you think it means when it refers to Jesus having "the power of an indestructable life"? What kind of power is this?
- Would you enjoy doing what your mom or dad does as a career? Pray that God will give you opportunities to share his love no matter what career you end up doing.

Day 3
Taking an Oath

Have you ever taken an oath? An oath is a solemn promise to fulfill certain duties. Boy Scouts take an oath to do their best to do their duty. When they enter office, politicians take an oath to uphold and defend the law. Doctors take an oath to protect and defend life. Some oaths are legally binding. A person who does not fulfill his or her oath has broken a promise and maybe even broken the law—but perhaps more importantly has let down those who placed trust in him or her.

Questions and Suggestions

- Read Hebrews 7:18–22. What oath did God make regarding Jesus? What does this mean?
- Thank God that the promise of Christ and his help in your life is sure—it will never fail!

Day 4
Hotline to Heaven

Into the 1980s there was an era called the "Cold" War, a time when the United States and the Soviet Union constantly threatened one another by stockpiling more and more nuclear weapons. It was called a "cold" war because no missiles were actually launched; it was the constant threat of a nuclear attack that kept things tense. During this time the president of the United States and the leader of the Soviet Union had a direct phone line to one another. They could just pick up the phone and be connected even without dialing. This instant communication was important because of the constant nuclear threat.

Questions and Suggestions

- Read Hebrews 7:23–25. Jesus and God the Father are constantly together—what do you think they talk about each day?
- Thank God that you can instantly and clearly express to him any need you have, since Jesus is there to intercede for you.

Day 5
Imperfect Pastors

God calls leaders in the church to higher standards. If you've ever read the books of 1 and 2 Timothy and Titus in the New Testament, you know this. These books were letters from Paul written to young pastors, and they contain instructions for what church leaders should do and how they should live. Even though pastors are called of God, they sometimes make mistakes. Sometimes they slip and fall. When we place our faith in people, we will be let down sooner or later. But Jesus the high priest never fails.

Questions and Suggestions

- Read Hebrews 7:26–28. When has someone in spiritual leadership let you down? How did that feel?
- Today, pray for those in leadership in your church, that God will keep them from sin and strengthen them for the work they are called to do.

Leading into the Session

Warm Up

Option 1 Have fun with science.
LITTLE PREP *Reproducible 1, pens or pencils, calculators*
Option 2 Learn the Eric Liddell story.
MORE PREP *Chariots of Fire movie and the necessary equipment to show it*

Starting Line

Option 1 Discuss great offers.
YOUNGER YOUTH *Newspaper or magazine ads, or Internet access*
Option 2 Discuss entrance requirements.
OLDER YOUTH *Chalkboard or dry erase board*

Leading through the Session

Straight Away

Explore the Bible passages.
Bibles

The Turn

Talk more about covenants.

Leading beyond the Session

Home Stretch

Option 1 Discuss completion.
YOUNGER YOUTH *Bible, comfy chair and footstool*
Option 2 Close the deal.
OLDER YOUTH

Finish Line

Option 1 See how we "live out the offer."
LITTLE PREP *Reproducible 2*
Option 2 Look at the power of blood.
MORE PREP *Lab technician or other authority on blood*

SESSION 3

CHRIST TO THE RESCUE!

Bible Passages
Hebrews 9:11–18; 10:11–18

Key Verse
He [Christ] did not enter by means of the blood of goats and calves; but he entered the Most Holy Place once for all by his own blood, having obtained eternal redemption.
—Hebrews 9:12

Main Thought
Christ will save all who accept his offer.

The heart's desire to stand clean before God runs through the pages of the Old Testament like a bright red thread. The psalmist celebrated the commandments. They are "more to be desired than gold, pure gold in plenty" because they "give thy servant warning" (19:10–11, NEB). The psalmist asked, "Who is aware of his unwitting sins? Cleanse me of any secret fault." (19:12, NEB). The sacrificial system of Israelite religion provided the means by which this request could be fulfilled. The faith of Israel lived between the desire to be clean and the "after-the-fact" cleansing of the sacrificial system. Sin offends God; it must be expiated and God's anger propitiated. By offering sacrifices ancient Israelites atoned for their sins and momentarily stood clean before God. However, that moment soon passed, and they would need to return and make sacrifice again and again.

The desire of the human heart is overmatched by God's desire for a people to stand before him without spot or blemish of any kind. The psalmist begged Israel to look to its Lord because "great is his power to set me free. He alone will set Israel free from all their sins" (130:4–8, NEB). The Old Testament looks to the day when the people of God will have a new heart. No prophet saw God's heart any clearer than Jeremiah, who declared that a new covenant with God was coming, not external but written on human hearts and minds. Hebrews quotes Jeremiah 31:33–34 to declare that the promised new covenant has come to be through Jesus' death on the cross. That he, the great high priest, is also the sacrificial victim that makes possible the new covenant is yet another mark of his exalted stature.

Israelite priests had gone about their duties for centuries with no discernable improvement in the people's faithfulness. Sacrifices cover sins already committed; they are a kind of payment after the fact. Jesus' sacrifice is qualitatively different in that he is the only priest who ever offered himself in atonement for sin; he is the only priest who *could* make such atonement. He is therefore the once-and-for-all sacrifice that abolishes the sacrificial system.

Jesus' death exalts him as the one-of-a-kind high priest and fulfills the ancient desire to stand clean before God. His sacrifice makes "perfect forever those who are being made holy" (Heb 10:14). We can now stand before God with perfection borrowed from Christ, even as the Holy Spirit continues working in us. God desires that we can stand before him and has graciously provided in Christ the answer to the psalmist's request that he be cleansed even from every secret fault. God also graciously makes available through Christ the power to answer one last request: "Hold back thy servant also from sins of self-will…. Then I shall be blameless and innocent of any great transgression" (Ps 19:13, NEB).

OPTION 1 (LITTLE PREP)

Have fun with science.

Distribute to the students copies of "Fun with Science" (Reproducible 1). Explain that the gravitational pull is different on different planets. This means that we would weigh more or less than what we weigh on earth if we were to go to Venus, Mars, or another planet. Give students time to calculate how much they would weigh on each of the planets listed; then discuss the results. Make some calculators available for the students to use as they complete this exercise.

Say, **Just as gravity grounds us and holds us in place on earth, we need a force to ground our faith and hold it in place.**

Warm Up

• •

OPTION 2 (MORE PREP)

Learn the Eric Liddell story.

Share the following story with your students (it is also available on the Digital BRIDGES CD as a projection):

Eric Liddell was born in 1902 to missionaries in China. He grew up as an avid runner and rugby player, and in 1924 he went to Paris to run in the Paris Olympics. When he learned that the 100 meter race would be held on a Sunday, he switched to the 400 meter competition because he wouldn't run on Sunday, the Lord's Day. He believed that competing on Sunday would break the commandment of God. He won a gold medal for the 400 meter competition and a bronze for the 200 meter. The movie *Chariots of Fire* is based on this part of his life.

Eric Liddell didn't want to break his spiritual covenant with God.

Show the clip from *Chariots of Fire* where Liddell is explaining his decision to the team officials. Start at approximately 1:28:45, where Liddell says, "I won't run on the Sabbath, and that's final." Stop at approximately 1:30:10, where Liddell says, "God knows I love my country, but I can't make that sacrifice." Afterward, discuss the following questions:

- **Do you think Eric Liddell was right in not competing on Sunday?**
- **Many amateur as well as professional Christian athletes compete on Sundays. Do you think they're doing the right thing?**
- **Do the people in our community (or our church) honor the Sabbath?**
- **How would things be different if we treated the Sabbath as Eric Liddell did?**
- **Do you think God honored Eric Liddell's faith when Eric won the gold medal, or do you think God was involved at all?**

Say, **Eric Liddell sought to honor his covenant with God by not competing on Sunday.**

> **Note:**
> If you sent the Portable Sanctuary home with students last week, take some time at the beginning of this session to review and discuss their experience.

> **Note:**
> For more information, see www.ericliddell.org.

Starting Line

Option 1 (Younger Youth)

Discuss great offers.

Bring to class newspaper or magazine ads promising things that seem too good to be true (lose all the weight you want, earn $10,000 a month, and so forth). If you have Internet access, surf the Web to find similar offers (take this survey and win a free iPod, click here to receive a $400 grocery certificate, and so forth). Discuss the outrageous claims of these ads. Ask, **What do you think would happen if you were to pursue these great offers?** Most of them require more than is obvious at first glance. Particularly with the Internet offers, you usually have to buy or sign up for something else before you get your "free" thing.

When you are ready to move on, say, **Let's look at a great offer that's the real deal.**

Option 2 (Older Youth)

Discuss entrance requirements.

Invite your students to share about different organizations, groups, or teams they have been a part of that have some sort of entrance requirements. As the students share what is required to be a part of each, list their responses on the board. Here are some possibilities to get thoughts going:

- *Sports teams or musical groups—a basic level of skill and knowledge of the game or instrument/music*
- *Academic clubs—a minimum GPA or interest in a certain subject*
- *Boy Scouts—completion of badge requirements, adherence to policies*
- *Sporting events and entertainment venues—payment of the entrance fees*

Ask, **What is the entrance requirement for a person to get into heaven?** That person must be holy and perfect, or must have his or her sins taken care of.

When you are ready to move on, say, **Let's look at someone who met the requirements to be in heaven—and makes it possible for us to get there as well.**

Leading through the Session

Straight Away

Explore the Bible passages.

Read together Hebrews 9:11–18 and discuss the following questions:

- **What is the "greater and more perfect tabernacle"?** The original tabernacle was a tent, a portable worship facility that the Hebrew people carried across the desert with them on their journey from Egypt to the Promised Land. It is where the people offered sacrifices to God in atonement for their sins. The greater tabernacle is the very presence of God.
- **What are the similarities and differences between the "earthly" tabernacle and the "tabernacle" of heaven?** The shed blood of animals was the sacrifice offered in the earthly tabernacle; the shed blood of Christ

was offered in the heavenly one. The blood of the animals took care of sins that had already been committed; the blood of Christ can clean the very heart and save us from death.

- **If we are under covenant with God, how can we still sin? Doesn't that break the contract?** Sin is a violation of the covenant. Through animal sacrifice the people could deal with their mistakes as they happened. But through the perfect sacrifice of Christ and the new covenant he offered, we can be free from sin. We might make mistakes sometimes, and we can certainly sin if we choose to, but in the power of Christ we are able to live without sin.
- **Why did blood have to be shed in order for these covenants to take effect?** The penalty for sin is death (see Romans 6:23). The lives of animals were sacrificed in the place of sinful human lives. The shedding of blood and the giving of life indicate that a covenant is a serious thing!

Read together Hebrews 10:11–18 and discuss the following questions:

- **What does it mean that Jesus "sat down at the right hand of God"? Was he tired?** Sitting indicates completion of the act, and the right hand was considered the position of honor. (HOME STRETCH, Option 1 [Younger Youth] looks more closely at this concept.)
- **What is different about a covenant that is written in our hearts and on our minds?** This is an internal thing, a part of us. It's not just a set of rules we obey; it becomes our way of life, changing our very nature from the inside out.
- **According to this passage, what perspective should we take on our past sins? God does not remember them anymore, so why should we?** Many times we have a tendency to "beat ourselves up" or experience recurring guilt over things we have done in the past. But if we have already asked God's forgiveness for something, he no longer remembers it.
- **If God completely forgives us when we ask, why do some people come back to Christ repeatedly to ask for forgiveness?** When Christ comes to reside in us, he stays there unless we boot him out. Just because we make a mistake doesn't mean he leaves us! As long as we walk with Christ, we should daily search our hearts for things that need forgiveness (see Matthew 6:9–13). Again, we don't need to beat ourselves up; we should get it right with God and move on.

Say, **Because of his perfect sacrifice for us, Christ offers us a relationship with God.**

The Turn

Talk more about covenants.

You may want simply to discuss the following description of God's covenant in the Old Testament with his people, or you could act it out with students pretending to be the various halves of the animals and doing the actions as you share the descriptions in your own words:

- A covenant is similar to a promise or a vow.
- When we promise something, we usually just give our word about it. A vow is a promise made either *to* God or with God as a witness.
- In the Old Testament, when people made a covenant they would dig a trench in the ground. Then they would take animals that they were sacrificing, cut them in two, and place one half on both sides of the trench. The blood from the animals would run down the sides and into the trench.
- The people making the covenant would make the promise to one another and to God while they were walking in the trench—in between the halves of the sacrificed animals. What they were saying figuratively was, "May I be cut in half like these animals if I do not live up to the promise I am now making!"
- The original covenant between the people and God had to be renewed every year with a sacrifice at the tabernacle or the temple. The covenant was broken when people broke the law of God.
- When Christ died and his blood was shed, he became the final sacrifice. He made a new covenant based on new promises.
- The new covenant is between Jesus Christ and God the Father. Jesus will not break the covenant and God will not break the covenant, so this covenant will last forever and will never be broken.
- If we find life and faith in Christ, then we are heirs to the covenant he made with God.

This can be a heavy concept; make sure your students understand how the new covenant is better. Invite them to ask any other questions they might have about this covenant. If you don't know the answers, find out and report back next week; or, bring your pastor in as a resource person.

Say, **Because of his covenant with God, Christ will save all who are willing to accept the offer.**

OPTION 1 (YOUNGER YOUTH)

Discuss completion.

Bring to class a comfy chair and footstool. You can either reveal them at this point or use them yourself throughout the session as your students enjoy their wonderful folding chairs. Share again Hebrews 10:12–13. Explain that the image of Jesus sitting at God's right hand and his enemies being his footstool symbolized three powerful things:

Home Stretch

- **Sitting symbolized completion. There was a finality to Christ's sacrifice for us. No one else needs to die for our sins or for the sins of anyone in the future; Christ did it all.**
- **Being at God's right hand symbolized honor. This was the best seat in the house, indicating the approval and favor of God the Father.**
- **Enemies as a footstool symbolized victory. Bowing to someone means submitting to this person; being a footstool is being under someone's feet—even lower! Sin and death are the enemy, and they have been defeated in Christ.**

This may be a good time to offer your students a chance to enter into the new covenant with Jesus Christ. You can do this as the Spirit leads and in the way that best fits your group. "Leading a Teenager to Christ" in the back of this book can give you some guidance.

When you are ready to move on, say, **Just as sitting in this chair requires faith that the chair will hold me, coming into relationship with God requires faith in Christ.**

• •

OPTION 2 (OLDER YOUTH)

Close the deal.

Explain that a covenant is usually proposed by one person or group to another person or group—kind of like a sales pitch. One of the first things a salesperson learns is to "close the deal." If you never ask the customer for a decision, you'll never be able to do any business. Say, **Here it is. You've heard about this new covenant. You know about the benefits of the covenant and the risks you take by not being part of the covenant. It's your choice whether or not to enter into this new covenant with Jesus Christ.** You can proceed from here as the Spirit leads and in the way that best fits your group. "Leading a Teenager to Christ" in the back of this book can give you some guidance.

When you are ready to move on, say, **God offers us life through the new covenant; we just need to accept the offer.**

Finish Line

OPTION 1 (LITTLE PREP)

See how we "live out the offer."

Distribute to students copies of "Living Out the Offer" (Reproducible 2) or show it as a projection and review together the information there. The goal is to give your students a clearer picture of what the tabernacle looked like, and to make the link to Christ and how we worship today. Here are some suggestions for how your congregation might experience each of the ancient worship elements in your weekly services:

- *Entering*—We gather in one place for worship, greeting one another as we come together.
- *Sacrificing*—We give an offering, sacrificing the best of what we have because we know God has blessed us with it.
- *Cleansing*—We pray to seek God's forgiveness.
- *Illumination*—As the Word of God is studied and taught, the light comes on; we understand it better and see ourselves and God more clearly.
- *Making an offering*—We offer ourselves to God in worship, not just an hour's worth but our whole lives.
- *Experiencing the presence of God*—God is present in a unique and powerful way when his people are gathered.
- *Being sent to minister to the people*—We go out from worship better equipped to love and serve those around us in the name of Christ.

Close the session in prayer, touching on each of these elements and thanking God for the new and eternal covenant offered to us in Jesus' name.

> *Note:*
>
> Don't forget to distribute copies of the Portable Sanctuary to students before they go.

- -

OPTION 2 (MORE PREP)

Look at the power of blood.

Invite to your group a lab technician, a nurse, or someone else who handles blood and is familiar with its function. If this individual could bring charts or other visual props, that would be great; part of the point is to make a good visual impact. Ask your guest to share about some of the precautions needed when handling blood, the benefits of blood, and the hazards of it. Point out that the blood of Christ would have looked just like anyone else's blood—red. Our blood has the power to keep each of us living, but the blood of Christ has power to bring eternal life to all who will receive it.

Close the session in prayer, thanking God for the power of the blood of Christ to save us and keep us for all eternity.

> *Note:*
>
> Be sure to thank your guest and to pray for him or her.

Fun with Science

On this sheet calculate how much you would weigh on each of the planets listed by multiplying your weight by the gravitational pull listed.

PLANET	YOUR WEIGHT NOW		GRAVITATIONAL PULL		YOUR NEW WEIGHT
Mars	_____	x	0.37	=	_____
Venus	_____	x	0.9	=	_____
Jupiter	_____	x	2.35	=	_____
Neptune	_____	x	1.12	=	_____
Saturn	_____	x	0.91	=	_____

Living Out the Offer

The original tabernacle was a curtained-off, open-air, rectangular-shaped court with a tent structure at one end of the court. Inside this tent structure was the Holy Place and the Holy of Holies. The priest would minister to and for the people in the court area on behalf of God; and he would minister to and for God inside the Holy Place and the Holy of Holies on behalf of the people.

Hebrews tells us that the earthly tabernacle was patterned after the heavenly tabernacle. In the earthly tabernacle, a worshiper would enter and offer a sacrifice. It would be ceremonially cleansed (washed), then the priest would enter the Holy Place and be illuminated by the light of the candlestick there. Once a year the high priest would enter the Holy of Holies and offer blood "for himself and for the sins the people had committed in ignorance" (Hebrews 9:7). The priest would then return to minister to the people.

The new covenant contains the same elements of worship. Can you identify how your congregation experiences each of the elements in your weekly worship?

- **Entering**
- **Sacrificing**
- **Cleansing**
- **Illumination**
- **Making an offering**
- **Experiencing the presence of God**
- **Being sent to minister to the people**

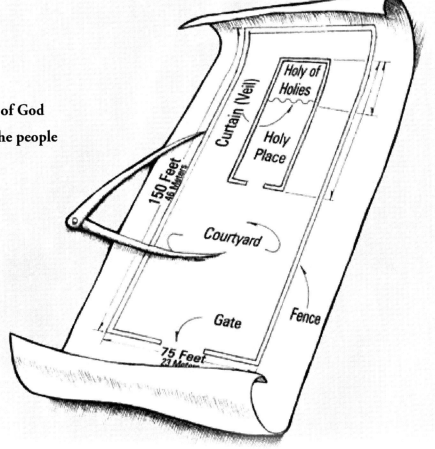

Portable Sanctuary

Day 1

Camping

Have you ever camped in a tent? When I was a kid, my family did this every summer at a park in the mountains. We would hike and fish in the day and sit around the campfire in the evening. There was no running water at the campsites. After being there for a few days, we would accumulate a good coating of dirt. The only option for a bath was an old tin washtub we brought. Tent camping was fun, but not fancy. God had a tent called the tabernacle—and it was fancier than any tent you or I have ever used!

Questions and Suggestions

- Read Hebrews 9:1–10. How much time do you think it took to set up and take down this elaborate "tent"?

- The things done and objects used in a worship service each have special meaning, even when we are unaware of it. Next time you're in church, notice what's going on around you and seek to understand what it means.

Day 2

An Earthly Shadow

What do you think heaven will be like? People sometimes talk of streets of gold and dazzling light; these are biblical images from the Book of Revelation. Sometimes people envision that we will float around on clouds and play harps; these are not biblical images. The Bible indicates that the earthly tabernacle is a shadow of the tabernacle in heaven. Heaven will be greater than anything we could ever imagine, but the earthly tabernacle gives us a clue as to how it will be to worship God in person.

Questions and Suggestions

- Read Hebrews 9:11–18. How can blood make anyone clean? What kinds of things has the blood of Christ set you free from?
- Pray that God will daily make you more and more ready to worship him in eternity.

Day 3
The Only Chance

If you've ever played on a sports team, you know that a season has a limited number of games. You will either win or lose (or maybe tie) them. If you've ever played in a concert and made a mistake, there's no erasing it; it's a part of history now. Once you die and your spirit leaves your body, that's it. Your skin grows cold and the cells start breaking down. Leaving our earthly body means entering eternity. The Bible indicates that eternity will begin with the judgment of God.

Questions and Suggestions

- Read Hebrews 9:19–28. What will you say at judgment in the presence of God? The blood of Christ is your only possible defense. Are you scared to face that moment? If Christ resides in you, you don't have to be.
- Pray that God will use you to share the good news of his new covenant with others.

Day 4
No Sacrifices?

It's nice when people give us gifts, but what kind of gifts can we give God? One of the gifts we can give is worship. A part of the people's worship used to be the sacrifice of animals. And yet there came a time when God said, "No more sacrifices!" He wasn't tired of the people's worship; it's just that their hearts weren't in it. They were going through the motions, but they needed an attitude check. God desires obedience to his will as our worship and sacrifice. It's better for us anyway!

Questions and Suggestions

- Read Hebrews 10:1–10. How is a shadow like the thing making it? How is it different?
- Thank God that he can do what you cannot—make you holy. He will do it if you ask.

Day 5
Day after Day

The longer you serve God, the more time you will spend at church. Even if you only go to a one-hour worship service each Sunday, that's still fifty hours of church a year—500 hours in ten years. If you also go to Sunday school and to Sunday night or Wednesday night church activities, the hours really start to stack up—hundreds in a year and thousands in a lifetime! Why keep going back? Because the Word of God is an endless source of truth and inspiration for our lives, and because our God is worthy of our frequent and eternal praise.

Questions and Suggestions

- Read Hebrews 10:11–18. Would you enjoy leading worship as your pastor does? Why or why not?
- If you think you might enjoy being a pastor or feel that God wants you to be one, pray about it and speak with your youth leader.

Leading into the Session

Warm Up

Option 1 Lay down the law.
LITTLE PREP Reproducible 1; copies of youth group guidelines (optional)

Option 2 Run a knee-ball relay.
MORE PREP Two soccer balls or volleyballs, a space large enough to run a relay race

Starting Line

Option 1 Discuss discipline.
YOUNGER YOUTH

Option 2 Analyze discipline.
OLDER YOUTH

Leading through the Session

Straight Away

Explore the Bible passage.
Bibles

The Turn

Discuss "blood-shedding resistance."
Bibles

Leading beyond the Session

Home Stretch

Option 1 Create a "cloud of witnesses."
YOUNGER YOUTH Reproducible 2, pens or pencils, tape
Option 2 Discuss future plans of discipline.
OLDER YOUTH

Finish Line

Option 1 Pray about hindrances and entanglements.
LITTLE PREP

Option 2 Throw off things that hinder us.
MORE PREP Paper, pens or pencils, creative place to discard things

---

SESSION 4

LOVING DISCIPLINE

Bible Passage
Hebrews 12:1–13

Key Verse
God disciplines us for our good, that we may share in his holiness.
—Hebrews 12:10

Main Thought
God's discipline is a good thing—it produces holiness in us.

Bible Background

Amid rival interpretations of Christ, the ancient Christian bishop Irenaeus declared that orthodox doctrine was taught, "everywhere, all the time, by everyone." Irenaeus lived in Lyons, France, and had no way of knowing whether all Christians were in theological agreement. Nevertheless he insisted that anyone teaching orthodox Christian doctrine had to conform to what he called the "rule of faith." This rule was an early form of a doctrinal statement later called the Apostles' Creed, one of the oldest doctrinal summaries in the Christian church. The Apostles' Creed refers to the "communion of the saints," the company of all believers in all places and times. When Irenaeus insisted that orthodox doctrine is taught "everywhere, all the time, by everyone" he was in effect appealing to the communion of the saints, a belief rooted in Hebrews 11 and 12.

Hebrews 11 is the great "faith chapter" of the New Testament. First, faith receives a textbook definition—"being sure of what we hope for and certain of what we do not see"—but then is further defined by examples of the great men and women of the Old Testament. From these heroes and heroines of faith chapter 12 shifts focus to the people for whom this discourse was intended, then and now. The image here is a race, but the race run by the church is not so much a sprint as it is a marathon or cross-country competition. In long races the runners reach the finish line utterly exhausted. If they have properly run their race they arrive at the end having used all the energy available to them; it is not uncommon to see cross-country runners being dragged away from the finish line to make room for those finishing behind them.

The church's race will take it through hardship, demanding perseverance of all its runners. But the church does not run alone. Surrounding it is the great cloud of witnesses, the communion of the saints, who have already finished and now cheer on the church like successful, encouraging teammates. Standing at the finish line is Jesus, who also has run this race but in a more demanding fashion than anyone ever faced. Hebrews instructs readers to keep their eyes on him, "the author and perfecter of our faith." He is the beginning and end of the race. That Jesus is the author of our faith means that we can enter the race only because of him. As faith's perfecter he has already finished, and is the complete example of how we are to run the race. Jesus is thus the Alpha and Omega, the beginning and the end of the great cloud of witnesses, the communion of the saints—witnesses who cheer us on and, by God's grace, witnesses we may join to cheer those coming on behind.

OPTION 1 (LITTLE PREP)

Lay down the law.

Distribute to students copies of "Youth Group Guidelines" (Reproducible 1) or show it as a projection, and review the information together. Discuss the following questions:

- **What do you think of these guidelines? Would they work with our group? Why or why not?**
- **What things would you add to this list? What things would you remove from this list?**
- **Do you think specific written guidelines are necessary or best for a youth group to have? Why or why not?**

If your own youth group has a set of guidelines, furnish copies to your students and discuss those guidelines specifically, including why they exist and the situations they seek to address.

Say, **Guidelines like this help to bring discipline to a group—and we all need discipline at times.**

OPTION 2 (MORE PREP)

Run a knee-ball relay.

You will need to run this activity in a room large enough so the students have to work to finish the race. You could even go outside to a yard or parking lot. Divide the group into two teams, and give each team some type of ball: a volleyball or soccer ball will work best. Ask the two teams to line up on one side of the room. The first person in line for each team must run to the other end of the room and back with a ball between his or her knees. The next person on the team can go when the previous one returns. The first team to finish the relay wins. Ask your students to be encouragers of their teammates.

Following the race, ask, **Does it embarrass you to run a silly race in front of other people?** Some students don't mind as much as others. It's not so bad when others are running the race with us.

Say, **We all run various races in life; with many of these races, the outcome is quite important.**

Warm Up

Note:

If you sent the Portable Sanctuary home with students last week, take some time at the beginning of this session to review and discuss their experience.

Starting Line

OPTION 1 (YOUNGER YOUTH)

Discuss discipline.

Discuss the following thoughts and questions:

- **Tell about a time when you were disciplined. What did you do that caused you to be disciplined? What were the consequences?** Steer the conversation toward funny anecdotes and away from griping about parents and other authority figures. However, be sensitive to those students who may have a rough home life. You may need to focus the conversation away from painful subjects. As always, be alert to potentially harmful situations and respond accordingly.
- **In what areas of your life do you *practice* discipline?** Help your students think about their involvement in sports, music, art, academics, and other areas in terms of discipline.
- **What are some positive results of discipline in your life?**

Point out that running the race of this life with Christ requires discipline. This means that we must both receive positive discipline from God and practice discipline in our daily lives.

When you are ready to move on, say, **Let's talk about what this discipline looks like.**

. . . .

OPTION 2 (OLDER YOUTH)

Analyze discipline.

Discuss the following questions:

- **When you hear the word *discipline*, what do you think of?**
- **Does the concept of discipline carry good connotations or bad connotations for you? Why?**
- **Think about *discipline* in the realm of a sport or art. Do your thoughts change at all? In what ways?**
- **In what areas of your life would you say you are disciplined? What does that look like?**
- **In what areas of your life would you say you lack discipline? Why?**

Point out that running the race of this life with Christ requires discipline. This means that we must both receive positive discipline from God and practice discipline in our daily lives.

When you are ready to move on, say, **Let's talk about what this discipline looks like.**

Explore the Bible passage.

Read together Hebrews 12:1–3 and discuss the following questions:

Straight Away

- **What metaphor is used in this passage to describe the spiritual life?** The metaphor is that of a race.
- **Do you think this race is more like a sprint or a marathon? Why or why not?** Help your students understand that this race is a marathon that starts when we come into relationship with Christ and ends only when we find ourselves in God's presence for eternity. It requires determination and energy for the long haul. Point out that many people start the race strong but burn out before they finish.
- **How is Jesus a good example for us in this race? How does he fit the metaphor?** Jesus is the author of our faith. He set an example for us by dying on the cross—he did not give up when things got tough, just as a marathoner does not give up when he or she gets a little tired. Jesus knew what his goal was and he persevered through the hardship because he knew the reward on the other side was great.

Read together Hebrews 12:4–13 and discuss the following questions:

- **What part of this passage is a little discouraging or depressing?** We have struggled, but not to the point of shedding blood yet! As Christians we can expect hard times—even discipline from God himself.
- **What word of encouragement are we given in this section?** We shouldn't get discouraged when we run into hardship or when we are disciplined by God. It only means that God accepts us as sons and daughters and he loves us enough to want better for us.
- **What is the connection in this passage between God's discipline and discipline from earthly adults who love us?** Just as a loving adult may discipline the child he loves because he knows the discipline is valuable, so our heavenly Father will discipline us. Point out that God's discipline may not be pleasant, but it should encourage us to know that God cares and is acting in our lives.
- **What is the ultimate purpose of discipline from our heavenly Father?** We undergo discipline so that we can share in God's holiness, righteousness, and peace. The discipline may be tough to go through, but it makes us better people, better Christians, and more holy like God.
- **Do you know anyone whose parents never discipline them? What are those people like?** "Spoiled brats" is a term we often use. Such people are often ungrateful for the things they have, throw a fit when things don't go their way, and have no skills or motivation to do anything for themselves.

Say, **God's discipline may not be easy, but it helps us succeed in the race.**

The Turn

Discuss "blood-shedding resistance."

Point the students' attention again to Hebrews 12:4. Discuss the following questions:

- **How did Jesus show this kind of resistance?** He put up with false accusations to the point where they took his life, and he died a very painful death as they pierced his hands and feet with nails. How easy it would have been to either plead his own case or call down the wrath of God on his accusers—and yet he resisted all the evil directed at him because he knew that *our* salvation depended on it.
- **When have others resisted opposition to the point of shedding their own blood?** Throughout history people have given their lives for things they believed strongly in. In 1989, students and other citizens in China protested the communist government, resulting in hundreds or even thousands of citizens being killed by the military. In 2007, protesters in Myanmar were murdered by government forces. These people knew the danger, yet they risked their lives because they believed in the cause.
- **Do you think you will ever have to resist something to the point of shedding your own blood?** In North America we live in one of the most peaceful and secure societies on earth. But nations have never lasted forever. Many in the world give their lives for their faith. Even if it's not to the point of shedding our blood yet, our faith is already challenged in many ways.

Say, **God's discipline can help us *now* when our faith is attacked or threatened.**

Leading beyond the Session

Home Stretch

OPTION 1 (YOUNGER YOUTH)

Create a "cloud of witnesses."

Hebrews mentions a "great cloud of witnesses" as an encouragement to us to successfully run the race of life. Distribute copies of "Cloud of Witnesses" (Reproducible 2). Ask, **Who first introduced you to Christ or the church? Who helps you *now* to grow in your faith? What examples can you think of from history of people who stood for the faith so it could be passed on to us today?** The students should write the names of these individuals on the handouts. Furnish tape and invite class members to post their "clouds" around the room. Spend a few minutes together looking at the names and discussing them. (These could include pastors, youth leaders, Sunday school teachers, family members, biblical figures, and others.)

When you are ready to move on, say, **These people experienced the loving discipline of God too—and now they stand on the sidelines and cheer us on.**

Option 2 (Older Youth)

Discuss future plans of discipline.

Invite your students to share about the discipline policies currently in place at their homes. Ask, **If you have your own kids someday, how will you discipline them? What will you use from your own parents' system? What will you do differently?** Share examples from your own childhood and your current family life. Point out that when we know that the one disciplining us loves us and cares for us, it makes the discipline easier to take. Discipline that is done with hatred or in anger brings fear, but loving discipline makes us stronger people.

When you are ready to move on, say, **God's loving discipline is a good example for us to follow in our own families.**

Option 1 (Little Prep)

Pray about hindrances and entanglements.

Invite your students to spend a few moments of self-reflection. Ask, **What are the things that hinder you from being closer to God? What are the things that entangle you and prevent you from being all God wants you to be?** Point out that the "stuff" in our lives is not always easy to overcome. If it were, we would just leave it behind and move on! Old habits are hard to break, destructive friendships are hard to leave behind, and many things that are pleasurable or enjoyable to us can suck the life out of us spiritually.

Finish Line

Close the session by praying that your students will be accepting of the discipline of God, and that their eyes would be opened to the awesome work he is doing in their lives.

Note:

Don't forget to distribute copies of the Portable Sanctuary to students before they go.

Option 2 (More Prep)

Throw off things that hinder us.

Distribute paper and pens or pencils and invite the students to spend a few moments of self-reflection. Ask, **What are the things that hinder you from being closer to God? What are the things that entangle you and prevent you from being all God wants you to be?** Point out that the "stuff" in our lives is not always easy to overcome. If it were, we would just leave it behind and move on! Old habits are hard to break, destructive friendships are hard to leave behind, and many things that are pleasurable or enjoyable to us can suck the life out of us spiritually.

Encourage your students to write down their personal hindrances and entanglements. Prepare or go to a place where you can creatively dispose of or destroy the papers. Some suggestions:

- Leave them on the altar.
- Toss them in the baptistry.
- Throw them in the trash.
- Put them in a trash compactor.
- Burn them.
- Flush them.

After you have disposed of the papers, close the session by praying that your students will be accepting of the discipline of God, and that their eyes would be opened to the awesome work God is doing in their lives.

Youth Group Guidelines

Here are sample guidelines from some different youth groups. What do you think about them?

- All clothing worn by youth and chaperones should reflect Christian Values. The S.A.L.T. test must be passed. S= too short, A= too alluring, L= too low, T= too tight. Anyone wearing clothing that is questionable will be asked to leave the function/ event for a change of appropriate clothing.
- Bathing suits must be appropriate for all youth functions where mixed swimming is present and must pass the S.A.L.T. test as well.
- The following items are NOT ALLOWED on any youth function at or away from church property:
  - Tobacco products of any kind
  - Alcoholic beverages, beer, or any other similar product
  - Knives, pistols, rifles, bows, or any other such weapon
  - No fighting
  - Skateboards, skates, or sporting goods that are health hazards and can cause injury
  - Profanity, obscene language, or vulgar language
  - Illegal drugs of any kind
  - Secular music, unless previously cleared with the youth pastor
- Show respect for everyone you come in contact with, by your actions and your words. This means that making fun of others and cutting each other down is not acceptable.
- Respect your brothers and sisters in Christ. An example would be, not to talk when someone else is talking.
- Respect the facilities. For example, do not throw or kick basketballs at the doors or walls.
- Keep a positive attitude.
- Remember that you are an ambassador for Christ and this church, and your actions and words can provide a good or bad example.
- No obscene language.

- No drug, alcohol, or tobacco use.
- Public display of affection with your significant other while at church functions is inappropriate. This detracts from our purpose as we meet together.
- Any videos or TV programs viewed shall have a G or PG rating.
- When rides to and from a church activity are being provided for the youth, at least one male and one female adult shall be in the vehicle.
- Consent forms shall be used for activities other than weekly activities that take place during church services, or monthly teen gatherings that do not include any special activities other than a social gathering.
- Adults seeking involvement in youth ministries shall submit background documentation and undergo a background check prior to being allowed to participate.
- Youth ministry leaders will make every effort to begin and end each event on time.
- Each person shall be respectful and attentive to others who are speaking during a group discussion.
- Inappropriate physical contact is absolutely not allowed, and those who inappropriately contact another person will be immediately warned or removed from the group as appropriate. (Inappropriate contact is considered, but not limited to, hitting, slapping, or any other physical contact that is harmful to the recipient. Patting someone anywhere other than the back-shoulder area is also considered inappropriate.)
- Any youth who are in a boyfriend-girlfriend relationship shall physically behave in the same manner toward each other as toward any other friend.
- No objects, including food, shall be thrown at another person.
- During church events where swimwear is worn, guys and girls are expected to wear appropriate swim trunks or one-piece swimsuits, and females wearing two-piece swimsuits are requested to wear an accompanying T-shirt.

Cloud of Witnesses

Who first introduced you to Christ or the church? Who helps you now to grow in your faith? What examples can you think of from history of people who stood for the faith so it could be passed on to us today?

Portable Sanctuary

Day 1

The Great Cloud

In the eighth grade I ran cross-country. I'm not sure why I did it. I didn't like to run, I wasn't built to run, and I wasn't a good runner. But I ran anyway. I consistently came in last place, whether there were two people in the race or twenty. (In one race I actually got a ribbon, because there were only five runners!) I was always dragging by the time I reached the finish line. But every time, my parents were there cheering me on. Their encouragement gave me the motivation and the strength to give my best and finish the race.

Questions and Suggestions

- Read Hebrews 12:1–3. What people have encouraged you or help you now in the race of faith?
- Today, thank God for the people he has put in your life, and ask him to make you an encouragment to others.

Day 2

Accepted Children

There used to be this kid at our church who was a total brat. He was rude, disruptive, and destructive. His dad was very touchy, and had this policy of, "No one disciplines my son except for me!" The only problem was, he never disciplined his son. Maybe his son thought, "Hey, it's great living this way!" But no one else thought that. This boy had a rough childhood, largely because of the way his dad disciplined him. The tension over this issue created problems in the rest of the family.

- Read Hebrews 12:4–6. What discipline from God has been the hardest for you to accept? Why?
- Pray that God will help you understand the discipline he gives you, and that he will help you to be a man or woman who gives discipline in a godly fashion.

Day 3
Leading to Something Good

Discipline as punishment and discipline as motivation are really not so different from each other. Our parents discipline us with the goal that we will learn consequences: If I do this thing, this other thing (punishment) will result. After a while, we learn not to do that thing. We discipline ourselves with much the same intention: If I do this thing, this other thing (benefit) will happen. The discipline is never pleasant when it's happening, but when it's over we have learned something—and we're better off than we were before.

Questions and Suggestions

- Read Hebrews 12:7–13. How has your parents' discipline of you changed over the years? What does this say about your maturity?
- Thank God for the reason he disciplines you—because he loves you and wants to make you more like him.

Day 4
Don't Miss Out!

When you're enjoying yourself, time just seems to fly; you wish you could stay in that place forever! When you're miserable, the time just drags; you wish the experience would be over! Heaven will be an eternal thing for those who go there—forever in the presence of God. God is holy. How miserable it would be to struggle with sin while living in the very presence of God! Holiness is necessary for us to experience the joy of eternity with our Creator. Without it, we cannot hope to see God.

Questions and Suggestions

- Read Hebrews 12:14–17. When have you missed out on the blessing of God because of bitterness or sin in your life?
- Submit yourself wholly to God, that he may make you holy.

Day 5
A Great Place

You may have heard it said, "No one could see God and live." God is all powerful (omnipotent), all knowing (omniscient), and present everywhere (omnipresent). That would be pretty overwhelming to anyone! How could we ever stand to be in the presence of someone like that? Because of the mediator Jesus. The blood of this perfect sacrifice can make us perfect in the sight of God. Heaven will be beyond anything we could imagine or expect—and we can go there because of Jesus.

Questions and Suggestions

- Read Hebrews 12:18–24. What's the most afraid you've ever been? What's the most joy you have ever known? Being in the presence of God is a stronger—and better—experience.
- As you pray and worship God, recognize his awesome holiness—and the joy of just being with him.

Leading into the Session

Warm Up

Option 1 Share a "leaving" story.
LITTLE PREP

Option 2 Conduct a "money loving" experiment.
MORE PREP *Reproducible 1 or Monopoly money*

Starting Line

Option 1 Entertain a stranger.
YOUNGER YOUTH *"New" person to visit the class*

Option 2 Analyze marriage vows.
OLDER YOUTH

Leading through the Session

Straight Away

Explore the Bible passage.
Bibles

The Turn

Discuss the statistics.

Leading beyond the Session

Home Stretch

Option 1 Exhort your students.
YOUNGER YOUTH *Church leaders to visit the class*

Option 2 Conduct a youth group exhortation.
OLDER YOUTH *Reproducible 2, pens or pencils*

Finish Line

Option 1 Discuss security reminders.
LITTLE PREP

Option 2 Distribute security reminders.
MORE PREP *Small scraps of blanket-type cloth*

SESSION 5

FOREVER WITH US

Bible Passage
Hebrews 13:1–16

Key Verse
Jesus Christ is the same yesterday and today and forever.
—Hebrews 13:8

Main Thought
We can be secure in Christ, our consistent, eternal Savior.

Bible Background

Jesus Christ is Savior. Jesus Christ is Lord. The first sentence is a theological claim and the second carries ethical implications for all believers. The text of Hebrews characteristically alternates between theological and ethical instruction; chapter 13 combines them in a series of concluding exhortations.

Love and hospitality are the first two virtues named in a list of several. None of them is optional for believers, a kind of spiritual frosting on the cake. Such virtues are character traits necessary for the proper functioning of the church's mission or purpose. Where would the church be without brotherly and sisterly love? The simile here reminds us that we do not select family members. We choose our friends on the basis of preferential love, but we have no choice when it comes to family. The church is the family of God; as in our earthly families, in the church "blood is thicker than water"—except that the blood shared by the church belongs to Christ. Similarly, hospitality encompasses a wider circle than preferential friendship, extending so far as to welcome strangers. That some have entertained angels unaware reminds us of the blessing that comes to the host who extends the blessing of hospitality to others.

The church first lives by memory rather than purpose-driven action plans. So Jesus instructed those who gather around his table to remember his death until he comes. Here in Hebrews the church is instructed to also remember prisoners and those who have been otherwise mistreated, presumably for the faith. The church's leaders are also to be remembered for their instruction by both precept and example. Hebrews also instructs its readers to live simply, be it in marriage (one partner only), money (do not fall in love with it), possessions (be content with what you have), or piety (grace internalized is to be preferred over external supports).

The theological foundation and goal of Christian character is Jesus Christ, "the same yesterday, today, and forever." Hebrews cannot conclude without one final reminder of the exalted stature of the church's great high priest. That he died outside the city of Jerusalem is a reminder that Christians are sojourners on earth; our citizenship, as Paul wrote, is in heaven, and it is toward the heavenly city that our lives here are to be oriented. Jesus, the scorned and sacrificed high priest, is the mediator through which our prayers ascend to God. Daily we praise God for his inexpressible goodness and grace in offering Christ for us, once again a point of theological instruction. Our sacrifice of praise is to be matched by doing good and sharing with others, another kind of sacrifice pleasing to God.

OPTION 1 (LITTLE PREP)

Share a "leaving" story.

Invite your students to share about the departure of the previous youth leader. How long ago did he or she go? How long had this person been with the youth group? What were the circumstances surrounding the departure? What is this person doing now? If your students have never had another youth leader prior to you, invite them to share about a favorite teacher from their childhood who had to leave. Ask, **Why do leaders whom we love and who are doing a good job have to leave sometimes?** There are family considerations and other circumstances in life that cause such changes. Sometimes leaders overwork themselves and get "burned out" (tired). Our leaders are not perfect and neither are we, so sometimes there are "people" issues that necessitate a change.

Say, **Even though they care about us, sometimes our leaders have to leave.**

Warm Up

Note:
If you sent the Portable Sanctuary home with students last week, take some time at the beginning of this session to review and discuss their experience.

• •

OPTION 2 (MORE PREP)

Conduct a "money loving" experiment.

Bring to class a set of Monopoly money; or, you can make copies of "Money Sheet" (Reproducible 1) and cut out the individual bills. Explain that you want to see who can collect the most money after you release it. At your count, throw the entire stash of bills in the air and let your students race to see who can pick up the most. (Take care that no students are hurt in the scuffle.) You can let the students keep what they grab, or else award it all to the person who grabs the most. (If you use Monopoly money, you will probably want to collect it instead!) Afterwards, ask, **How would you have responded if this were real money?** The effort to grab it probably would have been much more intense. Point out that it is bad if money has too high a priority in our lives, but money is necessary and helpful for us to live.

Say, **Money can cause trouble for us—but it is a necessary part of life.**

OPTION 1 (YOUNGER YOUTH)

Entertain a stranger.

This is an old teaching idea that your younger students may not be familiar with. Make arrangements for someone to visit the class whom your students do not know. If this could be somebody of their age, that would be ideal; but it could be somebody older, even an adult. Simply say "hello" to this person and nothing more; see how your students react to the guest. Do they talk, include, and try to get to know this person a little bit? After a time, introduce your guest and reveal that this person was a "plant." Ask, **Have you ever considered that a stranger you meet might have been sent to you by God—might even be an angel?** If time permits, share the following true story:

Starting Line

One time on our way to summer camp, our church van started acting up. We made it to camp okay, then my friend and I took the van into town

to try to figure out what was wrong with it. It was a weekend and no shops were open, and we didn't have any money to get it fixed anyway. We were in a parking lot with the engine running and the hood up, trying to decide what to do. Just then a man walked up and said, "It sounds like one of the spark plugs is loose. Sometimes you can just screw them back in." My friend and I weren't mechanics, but we started checking the spark plugs and found one that was loose. We hand-tightened it and started the engine again—and the van ran perfectly. We turned to thank the stranger for his advice, but he was gone—nowhere in sight. To this day we still wonder if it were an angel.

Point out that whether or not a stranger is an angel, such a person should be treated with the love of God—and may have something good to bring into our lives.

When you are ready to move on, say, **Let's see how angels, money, leaders, and many other things factor into our response to God.**

. . . .

Option 2 (Older Youth)

Analyze marriage vows.

Ask, **When you go to a wedding, what are the most common things you hear in the vows that the bride and groom exchange?** Invite the students to respond. A common pattern is something such as, "I, John, take you, Jane, to be my lawfully wedded wife, to have and to hold, from this day forward, for better or for worse, for richer or for poorer, in sickness and in health, till death do us part." Encourage the students to share about other statements they have heard in this context. (It used to be common that brides would pledge to *obey* their husbands, although this would be a point of controversy now!) Ask, **What is the whole point of wedding vows?** Even though various specific things are listed, they all contribute to a pledge of permanency. Two people are vowing to stay together for their entire lives, no matter what happens. Say, **Most couples make vows like this when they get married, and they mean them at the time. Why don't some of those couples make it?** The determination people have at first tends to weaken over time, and sometimes circumstances come up that were never imagined. Point out that making a "forever" pledge can seem easy when we are in the passion of the moment, but it's a lot tougher over time.

When you are ready to move on, say, **Let's look at a forever pledge that has held true for thousands of years.**

Explore the Bible passage.

Read together Hebrews 13:1–16 and discuss the following questions:

Straight Away

- **Is it easier to love a "brother" or a "stranger"? Why?** We tend to care more deeply about those we know best and are closest to. (We would quickly help out family members we love and our closest friends, but not necessarily strangers.) However, those we know best sometimes get on our nerves the most; strangers have done nothing to us that makes them difficult to love.

- **At your age, how can you help prisoners? How about the mistreated?** Youth students are probably too young to visit prisons; however, there are mistreated people all around us—and we should treat them as though we ourselves were receiving the mistreatment. It's easy for us to look away and say, "It's not my problem," but it takes guts to take up the cause of the mistreated and take action to bring them justice.

- **What does it mean to honor marriage and keep the marriage bed pure?** God has given the marriage relationship to us as a special gift, and it should be honored and protected. A "pure" marriage bed is one where the husband and wife are devoted exclusively to each other.

- **What does God's promise to never leave us or forsake us have to do with money?** Since we depend on money/income to live, many adults obsess over it, always worrying whether there will be enough and trying to make more. Those who know and depend on God's care might still need to earn a paycheck, but they don't need to obsess—God will always be with them and take care of them.

- **The writer of Hebrews quotes this question from the Psalms: "What can man do to me?" Well, what *can* other people do to us?** Christians are not saved from all troubles or harm, but we do not need to be afraid because of the threats we face. People can do a lot to us, including harming us physically and even taking our lives, but they cannot take away God's presence with us and assurance of eternity with him.

- **Hebrews warns us about "strange teachings." Have you ever heard "strange teachings" in school? When would they ever come up in the church?** Invite students to respond. If someone taught us things that we knew were wrong (e.g., there are only seven planets in our solar system, or Canada is the most populous country in the world), we would immediately reject those things. Some false ideas are more subtle. In the church, some groups teach "strange things" (e.g., the Mormons teaching that Jesus and Satan were brothers and that men can inherit their own planets in heaven someday) that have caused them to be labeled as cults.

- **Jesus died on a cross, a disgraceful death reserved for criminals. As his followers, how do *we* suffer and bear disgrace?** Many of the things the people of God stand for—marriage, caring for others, gathering for worship, and others—are disrespected and even ridiculed by the media and the public figures of our society. In many countries of the world, people cannot be Christians openly without facing persecution by the government and other religious groups. Jesus is the path to God—but he is not a ticket to an easy life!

• **How can someone continually praise Jesus and confess his name? Does this mean going to church every day?** We should be so close to Christ that his presence and his name are a part of everything we do. We should talk about him at school and at work, offer to pray for our friends, and keep a copy of his Word with us for quick reference. Ask students to suggest other ideas.

Say, **Because of Christ's eternal presence with us, we can be better friends, better spouses, better Christians—better people.**

The Turn

Discuss the statistics.

Point out how some statistical resources indicate that Christians make the same decisions in moral dilemmas as non-Christians do. For example, the divorce rate amongst Christians is similar to that amongst non-Christians. Similar percentages of Christians and non-Christians think it's okay to download "free" music and share it with their friends or to keep extra change that is given in mistake. Ask, **Statistically speaking, why do Christians behave the same as non-Christians? Why doesn't our faith make any difference?** You have been studying with your students the eternal power of Christ and the things he can do in and through us. If there is any problem, it must be with us and not with God! Point out that Christians are still human, and they still make mistakes. The words of Hebrews 13 conclude the whole book by exhorting (encouraging) believers to live in a way that *is* different.

Say, **The power of Christ can help us live differently; we'll never succeed on our own.**

Home Stretch

OPTION 1 (YOUNGER YOUTH)

Exhort your students.

Invite to your group some leaders from your church—pastors, board chairs and members, and so forth. Ask these guests to give positive exhortation and encouragement to your students. What do they see going on in the youth group that makes them proud? What do they appreciate about individual students? What advice would they give about how your students can stay strong and grow in the Lord? Let this be a good time to build relationships between your students and the leaders whom God has charged to serve the church of which your students are a part.

When you are ready to move on, say, **These men and women are here to support you and pray for you in your journey with the Lord.**

OPTION 2 (OLDER YOUTH)

Conduct a youth group evaluation.

Distribute to students copies of "Youth Group Exhortation" (Reproducible 2), go over the instructions, and allow time for the students to complete the handout. Emphasize that exhortation is usually of a positive and general nature; it's not listing the bad behavior of one or two people, but it is encouragement or guidance for the whole group.

After a few minutes, invite the students to share some of their thoughts and ideas with the rest of the class. What do they appreciate about the group? In what areas would they like to see it grow? What is the best thing they have received from the group? What advice would they give to middle school students—those who will be in the high school group in just a year or two?

When you are ready to move on, say, **Just as the writer of Hebrews did, we can also exhort and encourage one another.**

Finish Line

OPTION 1 (LITTLE PREP)

Discuss security reminders.

Invite your students to think of a favorite blanket or stuffed animal they had as a kid. Ask, **Why do many kids have blankets or stuffed animals?** These are items that bring security, a feeling of safety and well-being, especially at night or when a child is sick or worried. Ask, **What things do we turn to for security when we leave our blankets and stuffed animals behind?** We find security in friends, relationships, success, and possessions. Some people seek security through sex or through the effects of drugs or alcohol. As you have already studied, money (and a job that makes it possible) eventually becomes the main security source for many people. As children of God, we can have true and lasting security in Christ.

Close the session in prayer, asking God to fill your students' lives with the deep and lasting peace that only Christ can give.

> *Note:*
>
> Don't forget to distribute copies of the Portable Sanctuary to students before they go.

· ·

OPTION 2 (MORE PREP)

Distribute security reminders.

Ask your students if they are familiar with the *Peanuts* comic strip—Charlie Brown, Snoopy, Linus, Lucy, and so forth. Say, **Linus is well-known for one thing—what is it?** His blanket. Throughout the entire tenure of the comic strip, Linus always had his trusty blanket. Point out that blankets bring children security, a feeling of safety and well-being, especially at night or when they are sick or worried. Ask, **What things do we turn to for security when we leave our blankets behind?** We find security in friends, relationships, success, and possessions. Some people seek security through sex or through the effects of drugs or alcohol. As you have already studied, money (and a job that makes it possible) eventually becomes the main security source for many people. As children of God, we can have true and lasting security in Christ.

Bring to class some small square scraps of material that would be typical for a child's blanket. Give one scrap to each student as a reminder of the security that Christ provides. (The students might use these as Bible bookmarks or place them in some other location where they will be good reminders.) Close the session in prayer, asking God to fill your students' lives with the deep and lasting peace that only Christ can give.

Money Sheet

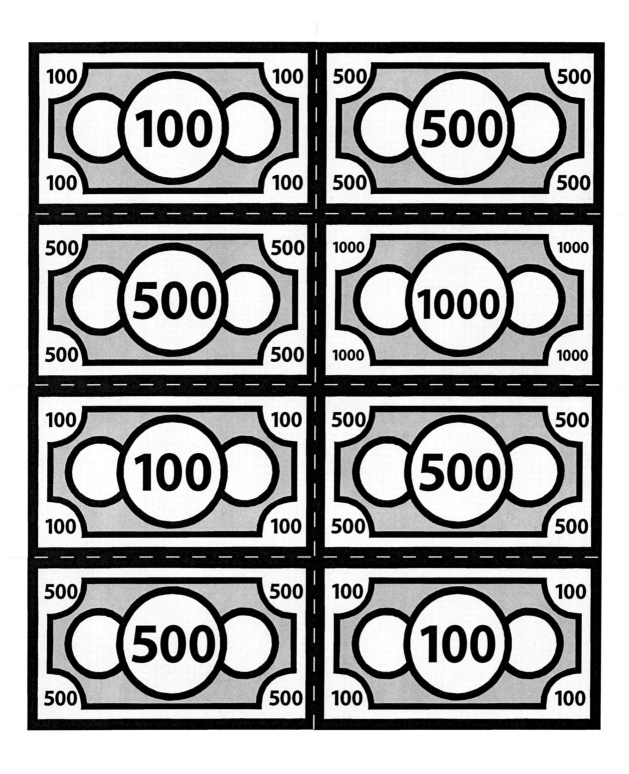

Youth Group Exhortation

Think about this class or youth group. What do you appreciate about it?

_____

_____

_____

_____

In what areas would you like to see this group grow or improve?

_____

_____

_____

_____

What is the best thing you have received from the group?

_____

_____

_____

_____

What advice would you give to middle school students—those who will be in this group in just a

year or two?

_____

_____

_____

_____

_____

_____

_____

Portable Sanctuary

NOTES

Day 1
Full Attention

Have you ever tried to talk with someone but gotten the distinct impression that he or she was not listening to you? How could you tell? The person was looking somewhere else instead of at you, or didn't respond when you asked a question. Maybe you were the one who didn't pay attention to someone else. Maybe you had a lot on your mind, or you were just bored. We can connect with people—even strangers—much better if we give them our full attention when we are with them.

Questions and Suggestions

- Read Hebrews 13:1–3. Do you welcome strangers and make them feel welcome? Is hospitality easy or difficult for you? Why or why not?
- Pray that God will make you more than hospitable—pray that he will make you an "angel" of his love to others.

Day 2
A Better Security

In North America we are truly blessed. Most of us have a roof over our heads, a bed to sleep in, clothes on our backs, and food to eat. We don't have to shop every day just to buy the meals for that day. In Jesus' day things were very different. People might have had homes and clothes, but there was no refrigerator or pantry stocked with food, and there was no checking or savings account. There would be food for the day if you went out and found a way to earn it or get it. But then or now, we struggle to find security. Jesus offers us that security.

Questions and Suggestions

- Read Hebrews 13:4–6. How can Christ make a person secure in marriage? in finances?
- Devote your future relationships and finances to God now, so you will be prepared to keep them pure and in the proper perspective.

Day 3
Faith Imitators

Whether or not you realize it, you are an imitator. The ways you talk, think, and act are influenced by the ways you have seen others talk, think, and act. Some of these people have been influencing you for years. In the future, new people will come into your life; they will influence you too. And just as you imitate others, there are some people who look at you and imitate you. You have already had a part in forming the speech, thoughts, and actions of someone else. How does that make you feel?

Questions and Suggestions

- Read Hebrews 13:7–10. Whose faith have you imitated? Whose faith did *those* people imitate? Do you realize that you are part of a "faith chain" that stretches all the way back to Christ?
- Pray that you will be a solid link to pass on the faith that was passed on to you.

Day 4
Going to the Dump

Have you ever been to a dump? It's basically a big pit in the ground where all of the city's garbage is taken and—well, dumped. When the pit is full, workers cover it up with dirt. In some countries the poorest of the poor live in dumps; it's the only place they can put a piece of tin over their heads for a roof and forage around other people's discards in search of food scraps. Dumps are located outside the city, and they are definitely not a place of honor. Jesus suffered dishonor outside the city

in order to make us holy. Are you ready to follow down that path?

Questions and Suggestions

- Read Hebrews 13:11–14. What place in your town or area is the toughest or most dishonored? How could Christ be honored there?
- Thank Jesus for the shame he bore—your shame and mine—so that we could be holy.

Day 5
Fruity Lips

We all know that the saying "Sticks and stones . . ." is not true. Words do hurt; many times they hurt even more than a physical assault. Bruises and broken bones mend, but the memory of hurtful words lingers. People who use their words to bless others and build them up instead of tear them down do a great thing. They put a smile on people's faces and joy in their hearts. Just think what could happen if you spoke constant blessing, or if you gave constant praise to God. People couldn't help but be pointed to the God you serve.

Questions and Suggestions

- Read Hebrews 13:15–16. What is the state of your "praise sacrifice"? Is it constant, nonexistent, or somewhere in-between?
- Spend some prayer time today in praise to God. Don't ask for anything or confess anything—just thank him for who he is and all he's done for you.

UNIT TWO

INTRO

Christ in the Gospels

CHRIST IN THE GOSPELS

Can you imagine trying to make sense of the rest of the Scriptures without the Gospels? The Old Testament points to Christ, and the epistles of the New Testament were written in response to Christ. The Bible is a united whole, and your students should read and study all of it. This unit will give them an overview of the narrative books that let us know what Jesus said and did.

Session 1 will focus on the power of Jesus as found in Luke. Session 2 will explore the healing ministry of Jesus as found in Mark. Session 3 will examine the servant leadership of Jesus illustrated in John. Session 4 will study Christ's decisive victory over sin as illustrated in Matthew.

May this unit help you and your students on the journey to know Christ more fully.

Unit 2 Special Prep

SESSION 1—WARM UP, Option 2 (More Prep), calls for the room, setup, and equipment necessary to conduct some strength competitions. For HOME STRETCH, Option 1 (Younger Youth), you can use an altar. FINISH LINE, Option 2 (More Prep), requires arrangements to pray for the need of a specific person or place.

SESSION 2—WARM UP, Option 2 (More Prep), calls for a visit to a place that is as quiet and isolated as possible. For STARTING LINE, Option 2 (Older Youth), you can use Internet access or pictures of skin diseases. FINISH LINE, Option 2 (More Prep), requires a guest to visit the class.

SESSION 3—WARM UP, Option 2 (More Prep), calls for white T-shirts and black permanent markers. STARTING LINE, Option 2 (Older Youth), requires various magazines. HOME STRETCH, Option 1 (Younger Youth), calls for construction paper, scissors, poster board, and tape. FINISH LINE, Option 2 (More Prep), requires pitchers of warm water, towels, and basins; you can also use some contemplative background music.

SESSION 4—WARM UP, Option 1 (Little Prep), calls for a blindfold. Option 2 (More Prep) requires the prior preparation of Reproducible 1. STARTING LINE, Option 1 (Younger Youth), calls for baby pictures of your students. For HOME STRETCH, Option 2 (Older Youth), you can have a guest dress up like Jesus. FINISH LINE, Option 2 (More Prep), requires time outside of class and Bible resources such as Bible dictionaries and commentaries.

Leading into the Session

Warm Up

Option 1
LITTLE PREP

Complete a word search.
Reproducible 1, pens or pencils

Option 2
MORE PREP

Conduct a power experiment.
Room, setup, and equipment for strength competitions

Starting Line

Option 1
YOUNGER YOUTH

Consider some "Catch 22s."

Option 2
OLDER YOUTH

Consider some statements about power.
Reproducible 2

Leading through the Session

Straight Away

Explore the Bible passages.
Bibles

The Turn

See how Jesus' power can help us.

Leading beyond the Session

Home Stretch

Option 1
YOUNGER YOUTH

Discuss altar calls.
Altar (optional)

Option 2
OLDER YOUTH

Discuss a modern-day deliverance.

Finish Line

Option 1
LITTLE PREP

Pray for Christ's power.

Option 2
MORE PREP

Be channels of the power of Christ.
Arrangements to pray for the need of a specific person or place

SESSION 1

THE POWER OF JESUS

Bible Passages
Luke 4:31–37;
20:1–8

Key Verse
All the people were amazed and said to each other, "What is this teaching? With authority and power he gives orders to evil spirits and they come out!"
—Luke 4:36

Main Thought
Jesus has power over any evil that can come against us.

71

Bible Background

Jesus did not graduate from an accredited rabbinical school, so to speak. Along with the content of his instruction his lack of credentials accounts for the amazement of his listeners. He was the son of a carpenter and had presumably learned the same trade at Joseph's side. In other words, Jesus was educated for life as a country craftsman and was quite without the religious pedigree of, say, a Saul of Tarsus. Jesus learned about wood and joints, whereas Saul studied with the rabbi Gamaliel. None of this is to suggest that formal education or academic degrees necessarily qualified men to become rabbis. In the first century the term was still honorary to some degree. Any teacher could be called "rabbi" as a mark of respect; in fact, *rabbi* means "teacher."

According to Luke 4, after Jesus announced the opening of his ministry in the synagogue at Nazareth he returned to Capernaum. It was not his first visit to this neighboring town; apparently he had healed people there during a previous visit. Back in Capernaum he visited the local synagogue where he taught on the Sabbath in the manner of a rabbi. While Jesus taught, a demon-possessed man cried out, but Jesus rebuked the demon and exorcized it from the unfortunate man. Twice this account notes people's amazed response to Jesus. In the first instance his authoritative teaching amazed the crowd; in the second it was his authority over demons and evil spirits. The early Christian bishop Cyril of Jerusalem observed of this two-fold amazement, "People who cannot be brought by argument to the sure knowledge of him who by nature and in truth is God and Lord may perhaps be won by miracles to a quiet obedience. Therefore helpfully, or rather necessarily, he [Jesus] often completes his lessons by going on to perform some mighty work."[1]

Jesus' opponents frequently raised questions about his authority. They surface again near the conclusion of Luke's Gospel during Jesus' final week in Jerusalem. While teaching in the temple he was approached by religious leaders who raised this familiar issue. Their question seemed to differ, however, from the question asked by members of the Capernaum synagogue. In Jerusalem the question of authority was not connected with amazement. The religious leaders were more interested in Jesus' credentials; they wanted to know who authorized him. Jesus rebuffed their question by putting them on the horns of a dilemma, asking their opinion whether the source of John the Baptist's authority was divine or human. Another ancient Christian commentator a generation or two older than Cyril, Ephrem the Syrian, observed:

> They [the religious leaders] began to reflect on it in their minds and to say, "If we [the religious leaders] say [Jesus' authority] was from heaven, he will say, 'Why did you not believe in it?' If we say, 'From human beings,' we are afraid of the crowd." When they said, "If it is from heaven" they did not also say, "We are afraid of God." They were thus afraid of human beings but not of God.[2]

1. Arthur A. Just, Jr., ed., *Luke,* from the series Ancient Christian Commentary on Scripture: New Testament, Vol. III (Downers Grove: InterVarsity Press, 2003), 84.
2. Ibid., 303.

OPTION 1 (LITTLE PREP)

Complete a word search.

Distribute copies of "Power Word Search" (Reproducible 1) to students and ask them to complete the assignment. The clues to the word search will provide some ideas about Jesus' power and give some hints about today's Bible study.

After the assignment is complete, ask, **Do these words give you a good idea of the power Jesus had?** Jesus was a powerful miracle worker, but he was also a powerful teacher.

Say, **Jesus did great things physically, but people were also amazed at the great truths he taught.**

Warm Up

• •

OPTION 2 (MORE PREP)

Conduct a power experiment.

Set up and conduct a few strength competitions for your students as time, equipment, and interest allow. Following are some possibilities:

• Set up a table and chairs and arm wrestle.
• Lift some heavy objects already at the church.
• Bring in a weight set for students to try.
• Have one-on-one tug of wars.

After your competition, ask, **What determines how much power we have?** Size is a big factor, but we can also exercise and train to gain more power.

Say, **Jesus had a lot of power—power straight from God.**

Note:

If you sent the Portable Sanctuary home with students last week, take some time at the beginning of this session to review and discuss their experience.

OPTION 1 (YOUNGER YOUTH)

Consider some "Catch 22s."

Ask, **What is a "Catch 22"?** This refers to a situation in which you can't win no matter what you do or which choice you make. Ask students to think of some "Catch 22s" they know of or have heard about. Here are some examples:

• **Let's flip a coin. Heads I win, tails you lose.**
• **You can't get a job without experience, but you can't get experience without a job.**
• **I need my keys to get into my house, but I need to get into my house to take my keys (because I forgot them).**
• **Can God make a rock so big that he can't lift it? If so, then God can't do everything. If not, then God can't do everything.**
• **If you won't let me cut in front of you in line, I'll get the person in front of you to let me cut in front of him, then I'll let him cut in front of me.**

Help your students to understand that it's impossible to respond to a "Catch

Starting Line

22." Some of them are tricks, but some are the result of a person's own mistakes or decisions.

When you are ready to move on, say, **Let's look at a time when Jesus used a "Catch 22" of sorts.**

. . . .

OPTION 2 (OLDER YOUTH)

Consider some statements about power.

Distribute to students copies of "Power Factor" (Reproducible 2) or show it as a projection. Review together the statements various people have made about power. Ask, **Which of these do you agree with? Which do you disagree with? Is power necessarily a good or bad thing? Why?** Explain that power can do much good, but it can do a lot of damage as well. When people possess power, the choice is largely up to them.

When you are ready to move on, say, **Let's look at the power Jesus had, and the way he used it.**

Straight Away

Explore the Bible passages.

Read together Luke 4:31–37 and discuss the following questions:

- **What does it mean when a message "has authority"?** When Jesus taught, the people knew that he meant what he said; he knew his subject matter well. The things he said were hard-hitting and made a difference in people's lives, and they "rang true" with the people.
- **Why would Jesus not want the demon in the man to speak?** By commanding it to be quiet, Jesus demonstrated his authority over demons. Also, the demon clearly identified Jesus' status as the "Holy One of God"; Jesus was somewhat guarded about his specific identity until later in his ministry. Just the act of casting out the demon was enough to spread the word of Jesus throughout the area.
- **What do we learn about Jesus' power from this passage?** It included teaching and the casting out of demons, it was instantaneous, and it was used to help people.

Now read together Luke 20:1–8 and discuss the following questions:

- **Jesus did a lot of teaching about God. What effect did it have in the long run?** Jesus drew large crowds whenever he taught; people got very excited about what he said. By the time of Jesus' resurrection and return to heaven, there was a core group of about 120 people who had received the message and determined to follow it. We can assume that many people who were excited at first did not let Jesus' message take root, although perhaps the seed was planted for them to respond to the message later. Point out that God calls us to share his Word; the success is up to God.

- **Why would the chief priests, teachers, and elders question Jesus' authority?** Teaching the crowds in the temple had been their territory. New teachers were usually trained by the veterans; Jesus had no such links. The leaders may have been motivated to question Jesus partly from genuine concern, but also out of jealousy.
- **Why did Jesus answer the religious leaders' question with a question of his own, almost a "trick" question?** Jesus taught with the same authority John the Baptist had—the authority of God. So, Jesus' question was closely related. Jesus knew that the real intent of the religious leaders was to get him in trouble, so he turned things around on them.
- **Why were the religious leaders "trapped" and unable to answer?** Many people had followed the teaching of John the Baptist, but the religious leaders had rejected him. If they admitted that John was actually sent from God, they would be condemning themselves and admitting that Jesus had authority from God; but if they said that John was not from God, they would make the people (who all loved John) upset.
- **What do we learn about Jesus' power from this passage?** Again, he was a powerful teacher; he also had the power to skillfully debate others and to know their hearts.

Say, **Jesus used his power to help others—by teaching them and by dealing with the demons in their lives.**

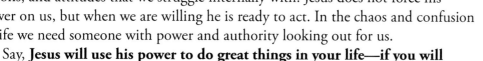

See how Jesus' power can help us.

Say, **Jesus did some great teaching and cast out some demons when he was here. How can that help us now?** Invite students to respond. The teaching of Jesus has continued to change lives for two thousand years; all that your youth group and church does is based on that same teaching. Demons are servants of Satan, a direct link to evil; Jesus still has power over any evil that might come against us. This includes people or situations that might harm us, but it also includes thoughts, actions, and attitudes that we struggle internally with. Jesus does not force his power on us, but when we are willing he is ready to act. In the chaos and confusion of life we need someone with power and authority looking out for us.

Say, **Jesus will use his power to do great things in your life—if you will invite him to do so.**

The Turn

Home Stretch

OPTION 1 (YOUNGER YOUTH)

Discuss altar calls.

Ask, **What is an altar?** If possible, have an altar present for today's session. Originally, an altar was a place where a burnt offering was sacrificed; it was often made of stones. In the Old Testament we read of certain altars that continued on as memorials to God after their initial use. Certain churches today might refer to the area where the Communion elements sit as an altar. Many church groups have applied the altar concept to the kneeling benches in front of the church where people go for prayer; the idea is that we sacrifice our own wills and give our lives as an offering to God as we kneel to seek God's power and help. Discuss the use of altars in your church. Point out that going to an altar is not required to meet God or make a spiritual decision, but the public act of taking that walk brings support from others. An altar is a great place to seek God's power and to invite Jesus to work in our lives.

When you are ready to move on, say, **If you haven't knelt at an altar before, give it a try. It's a place that all Christians can benefit from regularly using.**

. . . .

OPTION 2

Discuss a modern-day deliverance.

Discuss the following true story with your students. It comes from Dr. Maxie Dunnam, former president of Asbury Theological Seminary:

Note:

See Frank Bateman Stanger, *God's Healing Community* (Nappanee, Ind.: Evangel Publishing House, 2000), 8-9

> **I have witnessed [Christ's healing power] dramatically. I remember a young woman—this young woman had been sexually abused as a child by her father....**
>
> **She was under psychiatric care as well as pastoral care from ministers in our congregation. I noticed that she always kept her distance from me....**
>
> **I will never forget an experience ... at our evening worship—which was a service of celebration, praise, holy communion, and healing prayer—[when] we invited people to come to the altar for specific prayer.... She almost ran across the front of the church and knelt before me. It was obvious that a power not her own was propelling her. She reached out to take my hands. Before that night, she would not have gotten within five feet of me. I prayed and she began to pray. Her prayer exorcised the spirits of shame and guilt and depression, the feelings of worthlessness and uncleanness that had come from being violated. The Holy Spirit prevailed over the negative emotions that had been ruling her life. The Holy Spirit prevailed, because the love of Jesus Christ had been expressed through some pastors and an able and understanding therapist who cared for her.**

Ask, **Do you agree that this woman's healing was a kind of "exorcism"? Have you known anyone who was miraculously healed of such a disorder?** Invite students to respond. We often think "exorcism" refers only to demonic spirits, but anyone who's been healed of serious mental or emotional illness would say their experience was just as marvelous. Let's praise God for these kinds of deliverance as well.

When you are ready to move on, say, **Whether it's a demon or some other influence exercising power over you, the power of Christ is greater.**

Finish Line

Option 1 (Little Prep)

Pray for Christ's power.

Invite students to reflect silently on the following questions:

- **How active is the power of Christ in your life? Are you open to his teaching and deliverance, or have you grown cold and fallen under the spell of the enemy?**
- **Where are you struggling in your walk with God? What is it that you most want Christ to teach you?**
- **Are there any habits or attitudes you're struggling with right now? Are you willing to give those to Christ so their power over you can be broken?**

Close the class with prayer, thanking God for the power of Christ to break the strongholds in our lives and bring us victory. Invite any students who are struggling with personal issues to speak with you privately.

Note:

Don't forget to distribute copies of the Portable Sanctuary to students before they go.

Option 2 (More Prep)

Be channels of the power of Christ.

Say, **Jesus has commissioned his followers to minister as he did. John 14:12 says that we will do even greater things than Christ!**

Find out about a specific prayer need in your church or community. Perhaps there is an individual in the congregation who is sick or dealing with some heavy issues. Maybe there is an organization in town that is seeking to serve the Lord but has met with tough opposition. Identify a person or situation where the power of Christ is really needed right now and make arrangements for your group to pray for that need by either going to the person or place or else by bringing the person to your class. If you pray for a person, you may wish to anoint him or her with oil as James 5:13–16 commands and invite your students to offer prayers that the power of Christ would make a positive difference in that person's life. If your subject is a place, conduct a "prayer walk" around it as your students seek the intervention of the power of Christ.

Close the session by inviting the power of Christ to break the enemy's power in your students' lives as they submit to God.

Power Word Search

See if you can find the words at the bottom of the page in the following puzzle. These words will get you thinking about today's topic.

```
E   N   E   R   G   Y   X   P   Q   U   P   M

E   U   G   O   G   A   N   Y   S   H   R   Y

T   P   R   O   P   H   E   T   A   M   I   T

L   N   D   J   R   T   E   M   P   L   E   I

C   E   M   L   O   G   R   H   B   U   S   R

R   W   S   B   I   N   T   L   H   Y   T   O

N   S   N   O   M   E   D   A   V   P   S   H

H   D   E   U   A   R   Z   M   R   W   I   T

O   A   T   C   S   T   K   E   A   X   D   U

J   E   H   J   L   S   Y   L   F   C   N   A
```

ENERGY	DEMONS	PRIESTS
STRENGTH	NEWS	LAW
TEACH	TEMPLE	JOHN
AUTHORITY	SYNAGOGUE	PROPHET

Power Factor

Consider each of the statements below about power. Which do you agree with? Which do you disagree with? Is power necessarily a good or bad thing? Why?

 The way to have power is to take it.—*Boss Tweed*

 Fight the power that be. Fight the power.—*Spike Lee*

 The most important thing about power is to make sure you don't have to use it.—*Edwin Land*

 You have no power at all if you do not exercise constant power.—*Major Owens*

 Use power to help people. For we are given power not to advance our own purposes nor to make a great show in the world, nor a name. There is but one just use of power and it is to serve people.—*George W. Bush*

 Power tends to corrupt, and absolute power corrupts absolutely.—*John Acton*

 Power is of two kinds. One is obtained by the fear of punishment and the other by acts of love. Power based on love is a thousand times more effective and permanent than the one derived from fear of punishment.—*Mohandas Gandhi*

 Power has no limits.—*Tiberius*

 Do not pray for easy lives. Pray to be stronger men! Do not pray for tasks equal to your powers. Pray for power equal to your tasks.—*Phillips Brooks*

 Power will intoxicate the best hearts, as wine the strongest heads. No man is wise enough, nor good enough to be trusted with unlimited power.—*Charles Caleb Colton*

Portable Sanctuary

Day 1
Distant Power

Jesus touched and healed many people. One time a man came to Jesus to seek healing for his servant, who was sick at home. Jesus was prepared to go with the man, but the man said, "That's not even necessary! Just say the word from here and my servant will be healed." Jesus was amazed at the man's faith, and he healed the servant long distance. The power of Christ is so great that it can reach across the miles to heal, free, and restore.

Questions and Suggestions

- Read Matthew 8:5–13. What were the keys to this healing taking place? What did authority have to do with it?
- Never be afraid to pray for any need or any person, even if that person is far away from you. Nothing is impossible for God!

Day 2
Accountable Power

In North America, our governmental systems are set up with what we call "checks and balances." They have different sections that each do different things. The power is "spread around" on purpose so that one individual or group doesn't control everything. In some nations, one person runs the whole show. This is called a "dictatorship." In these cases it's not long before this ruler runs the media, lives extravagantly while most of the people are poor, and takes military steps against his own people to make sure he stays in power as long as he wants.

Questions and Suggestions

- Read John 5:16–30. According to this passage, where does Jesus get his power? What guides the use of that power?
- Pray that God will use your connection with him to bring the healing power of Christ to the lives of others.

Day 3
Compassionate Power

A young man named Joseph was the victim of jealousy. His brothers sold him into slavery, and then told their father that he had been killed. God blessed Joseph, and over time he became wealthy and powerful. Later on, these same brothers came back into Joseph's life. Even though Joseph had the power and the chance to take revenge on his brothers, he didn't. Instead, Joseph felt compassion deep inside his heart when he saw his brothers again after all those years.

Questions and Suggestions

- Read Genesis 42:1—43:30. How did Joseph show compassion? What *could* he have done with his power?
- Pray that God will fill you with compassion for others, even those who might not deserve your compassion.

Day 4
Power to Heal

In order to be missionaries, people leave their families, friends, and good jobs behind. Many of them sell their homes, their furniture, and all their possessions before leaving for the missionary field. Many of these people have to raise most or all of their own financial support. Being a missionary is not a path to getting rich, a better job, or an easier life. Yet thousands of people make this choice every year. Why do they do it? Because God calls them to share his love and healing power—and they are willing to go.

Questions and Suggestions

- Read 1 Corinthians 9:16. How passionate was Paul about God's calling on his life?
- Even if you don't become a doctor and don't have the gift of miraculous healing, pray that God's healing power will flow through you to everyone you meet.

Day 5
Feeling the Power

Have you ever noticed that the lights in your house dim whenever you turn on the hair dryer? It's because these devices use a lot of electrical power for their heaters. When all that power is going to the hair dryer, there is less of it available to go to the lights. When one circuit in a house uses too much power, it blows a fuse or trips a circuit breaker. When a city or area uses too much power, it can cause a power outage for thousands and thousands of people.

Questions and Suggestions

- Read Mark 5:21–43. Do you think Jesus really didn't know who touched him? Why was it important to ask?
- Remember, a kind touch and caring words can be powerful ways to share the love of Christ.

Leading into the Session

Warm Up

Option 1 List ways we care for others.
LITTLE PREP *Paper, pens or pencils*
Option 2 Go to a solitary place.
MORE PREP *Place that is as quiet and isolated as possible*

Starting Line

Option 1 Play Bible charades.
YOUNGER YOUTH *Bibles, Reproducible 1*
Option 2 Study leprosy.
OLDER YOUTH *Reproducible 2; Internet access or pictures of skin diseases (optional)*

Leading through the Session

Straight Away

Explore the Bible passage.
Bibles

The Turn

Identify points of need.

Leading beyond the Session

Home Stretch

Option 1 Experience the discipline of silence.
YOUNGER YOUTH

Option 2 Discuss the power of the will.
OLDER YOUTH

Finish Line

Option 1 Pray for specific needs.
LITTLE PREP

Option 2 Listen to a testimony and pray.
MORE PREP *Guest to visit the class*

SESSION 2

JESUS THE HEALER

Bible Passage
Mark 1:29–45

Key Verse
Filled with compassion, Jesus reached out his hand and touched the man. "I am willing," he said. "Be clean!"
—Mark 1:41

Main Thought
Jesus touched people at their point of need.

Bible Background

Tradition names four ancient doctors of the western, Latin-speaking church. "Doctor" in this case means "teacher," from the same Latin root from which also comes our word "orthodox"—literally, "straight teaching." One of the four Latin ancient doctors was a man named Jerome, one of the greatest Bible scholars of all time. Famous for his grouchy, reclusive temperament, Jerome nevertheless was and remains widely admired for his knowledge of the Bible and his skill in interpretation. He lived from about AD 347 to 420, making him a contemporary of the great Augustine, another of the four ancient western doctors. Jerome's greatest achievement was his monumental translation of the Bible, the Vulgate edition. He mastered Greek and Hebrew (a language mostly unknown to Latin-speaking Christians), and prepared a fresh new translation into Latin. Today only scholars and college prep high school students read Latin, but in the fifth century it was the common (in Latin, "vulgar") language, hence the name of Jerome's brilliant work. The Vulgate Bible was virtually the only Bible in the western church for a thousand years.

Jerome was an insightful interpreter of the Bible as well as the author of its most enduring translation. Of the healing of Simon's mother-in-law he commented, "Can you imagine Jesus standing before your bed and you continue sleeping? It is absurd that you would remain in bed in his presence. Where is Jesus? He is already here offering himself to us."[1] In these early verses of Mark's Gospel Jesus is not difficult to find. He can be seen regularly in synagogues in Nazareth and Capernaum or walking along the Sea of Galilee. Ancient Mediterranean peoples spent much of their time outdoors, so crowds could find him rather easily, even when he sought solitude in "lonely places." Galilean houses were small, particularly those owned or rented by the "people of the land." They were places for eating and sleeping; socializing was an outdoor activity, but Jesus entered houses when invited or when a need arose. Jerome asks, "Where is Jesus?" and in so many words the text answers, "Anywhere." Jesus is the incarnate rule and reign of God, the *autobasileia*—the "kingdom in person"—as another early Christian interpreter, Origen, called him, and the Kingdom is among you. Jesus is among the people, on their roads, in their towns, and even in their bedrooms. Where he is present the good news of the Kingdom is manifest and it cannot, it will not be suppressed. The word spreads: a sick lady is healed, demons are cast out, a leper is restored to health and society. That kind of news will attract a crowd, and so all kinds of needy people look for this rabbi who, Mark tells us, is filled with compassion. Into Galilee's villages and countryside has come an extraordinary man who wants to help and possesses power to do so. Suddenly he is at your bedside, taking your hand. Who indeed could stay in bed in the presence of such a man? Who could keep secret his powerful, compassionate acts?

1. Thomas C. Oden and Christopher Hall, ed., *Mark,* from the series Ancient Christian Commentary on Scripture: New Testament, Vol. II (Downers Grove: InterVarsity Press, 1998), 24.

OPTION 1 (LITTLE PREP)

List ways we care for others.

Ask your students to get into small groups and list ways that a person expresses concern for others. One person in each group should serve as recorder. Emphasize to your students that not only in the big things can we express caring but also in the everyday aspects of life. Caring is an important criterion used when we evaluate our friendships and relationships. It doesn't take long for persons to know if someone really cares for them. The saying "People don't care how much you know until they know how much you care" is true.

After a few minutes, bring the class together and allow each group the opportunity to express the examples of caring they have listed. Note ones that are commonly shared by the groups and ones that are distinctly different.

Say, **We gain a sense of value and importance when we know that someone cares for us.**

Warm Up

Note:
If you sent the Portable Sanctuary home with students last week, take some time at the beginning of this session to review and discuss their experience.

• •

OPTION 2 (MORE PREP)

Go to a solitary place.

Take your students to the most quiet and isolated place possible. This may be a room in the church or home where you meet, a nearby location outdoors, or something else. The quieter the place, the better. Allow your students to experience the silence for a few minutes; then discuss the following questions:

• **Even though this place is isolated and quiet, what things do you still hear?**
• **Do you enjoy being in quiet places like this, or does it drive you crazy?**
• **What good is a quiet place like this? What useful thing could you possibly do here?** If we need to focus our thoughts (for study, prayer, or something else), a quiet place can sometimes be helpful.

Say, **Quiet places can be good things at certain times in our lives.**

OPTION 1 (YOUNGER YOUTH)

Play Bible charades.

Divide the class into small groups. Make copies of "Bible Charades" (Reproducible 1), cut them apart, and give one slip to each group. (If necessary, you can use multiple copies and give the same slips to different groups.) The students should look up the scriptures and work in their groups to come up with skits that demonstrate how God's caring is portrayed. Encourage each group to utilize all the members in the performance of the skit. Here are the situations that should be portrayed:

• Genesis 3:6–8, 21 (God made clothing for Adam and Eve.)

Starting Line

- Genesis 6:9–14 (God saved Noah and his family from the flood.)
- Exodus 13:17–22 (God led the Israelites through the desert by a pillar of fire and cloud.)
- Joshua 6:1–20 (God gave the Israelites victory at the city of Jericho.)
- Jonah 4:5–6 (God provided a vine to grow and shade Jonah.)
- Matthew 17:24–27 (God provided money for Jesus and Peter to pay the temple tax.)
- John 6:1–13 (God multiplied food to feed a hungry crowd.)
- Acts 4:32–35 (God provided for his people by the generosity of the whole group.)

After all the skits have been presented, point out that God has always taken the initiative to show people he cares for them. Throughout the Bible we find a common thread: God constantly initiates relationships with persons and with groups of people. The idea of relationship is what makes Christianity unique when compared to other religions. God does give us guidelines, but the goal is a personal relationship with him.

When you are ready to move on, say, **Let's see how Jesus touched people at their point of need.**

. . . .

OPTION 2 (OLDER YOUTH)
Study leprosy.

Distribute to students copies of "Leprosy Then and Now" (Reproducible 2) or show it as a projection. Review together the technical aspects of leprosy, the way it was dealt with in Bible times, and the ways it is treated now. If possible, go online or bring in color pictures that can more graphically demonstrate the destruction and suffering caused by skin diseases. Point out that because North Americans are so far removed from this disease today, it can be difficult for us to understand the negative stigma that is often associated with it. Ask, **How do you react when you see someone who looks as if they have some catching disease, or smell someone who is stinky?** We tend to distance ourselves from people who might be "contagious" because we don't want to catch what they have.

When you are ready to move on, say, **Let's see how Jesus ministered to a man who was suffering with leprosy.**

Explore the Bible passage.

Read together Mark 1:29–45 and discuss the following questions:

Straight Away

- **Compare the other Gospels (Matthew, Luke, and John) with Mark. How soon does Jesus "get busy" in each?** Matthew and Luke tell of Jesus' birth; Jesus is not a grown man doing ministry until a few chapters in. In John, Jesus' first miracle was changing water to wine at a wedding feast (2:1–11), but he acted as if it was too early for him to be doing miracles. Mark has Jesus getting right to business in the first chapter; Jesus is an active teacher and miracle-worker.

- **How did Simon's mother-in-law respond to being healed of her fever?** She got up and began to wait on her guests. Such hospitality was expected in that culture.

- **What variety of needs did Jesus respond to while he was at Simon and Andrew's house?** He healed a fever and "various diseases," and drove out demons. Whatever the need was, Jesus took care of it.

- **Why do you think Jesus got up early to go off by himself and pray?** Doing ministry is hard work! People were always wanting to be with Jesus, to learn from him or be healed by him. A few moments alone in the morning may have helped "recharge his batteries." Jesus frequently took time to be alone with God because he knew how important it was. For *any* of us, prayer is a good way to prepare for the stress of the coming day.

- **Why did Jesus move on from Simon and Andrew's town?** He felt it was important to minister in other places too. Point out that each of us is a part of God's plan. No one is the answer to it all; no one can fix every problem that comes along. In the church and in life, people come and go as God directs. We need to be sensitive to where the Spirit of God is leading us.

- **What strikes you about Jesus' healing of the man with leprosy?** The man submitted to Jesus' will. Jesus felt compassion for the man—he truly felt bad for the man's condition and wanted to help. Jesus touched a person who was considered highly infectious. The man probably hadn't been touched by anyone in years. The physical contact was probably just as important as the healing itself.

- **What does being healed have to do with being "clean"?** According to Old Testament law, having an infectious skin disease made a person "unclean." Such a person had to stay outside of town until the person proved to the priest that he or she was better. In the case of a leper, the person would never get better. There were other conditions (such as bleeding or coming in contact with a dead person) that could also make a person "unclean."

- **What did Jesus warn the man to do—and what happened instead?** Jesus told him not to tell anyone about the healing. Instead, the man spread the news—and Jesus was basically mobbed by fans.

Say, **Whether the need was knowledge, healing, or casting out demons, Jesus was there to meet the need.**

The Turn

Identify points of need.

Ask, **Anyone with leprosy in here? How about demons? What does today's story have to do with Jesus' work in *our* lives?** Invite students to respond. There are still people in the world today who suffer from leprosy, and others who suffer from demon possession. Explain that Jesus touched people at their point of need—whatever the point happened to be. Invite students to share about points of need that are common today. For example, someone might battle drug or alcohol addiction. Jesus can heal that. Someone might be dealing with divorce. Jesus can bring healing. Physical needs are certainly still covered by Jesus' healing power. Whatever needs people had, they brought them to Jesus—and Jesus took care of them. This is still the case.

Say, **Jesus will help you, your family, and your friends at whatever your point of need might be.**

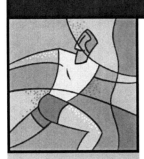

Home Stretch

Option 1 (Younger Youth)

Experience the discipline of silence.

Point out that Jesus' time in a solitary place seemed to refresh him from the ministry he had just done and prepare him for the ministry he was about to do. Give students some "silent time" to think of needs in their lives. If you wish, you can allow them the freedom to go someplace in the building or outside to spend their silent time. Explain that the needs they think of do not necessarily have to be physical in nature. They may be carrying damaged emotions or thoughts, for instance. God's Holy Spirit is more than capable to bring wholeness and healing to every need. Students should remain totally silent for this time. Explain that silence takes discipline at first, but it can allow us to hear things from God that we might have missed before. After your silent time is through, let students know that you are available after class if they need to discuss any issues in their lives.

When you are ready to move on, say, **Times of silence with God can be very good for your spiritual health.**

· ·

Option 2 (Older Youth)

Discuss the power of the will.

Say, **It has been said that the only difference between successful people and unsuccessful people is that successful people are willing to do what unsuccessful people are not willing to do. What do you think this means?** We can always study harder, work harder, wait longer, practice longer, make more phone calls, or do whatever to get ahead at something. Someone who is willing to work twenty hours a day could make lots of money (but wouldn't have the time or energy to enjoy it!). Ask, **What is something you could do if your will was strong enough?** Invite students to respond. The power of the human will is amazing. It drives starving or sick people to survive. It drives people to climb dangerous mountains and perform other incredible feats. Now ask, **Can we do *everything* we will (or want to)?** No; there are limits to what we can do. Point out that in the case of Christ, he can do anything he wills—and he wills only what God the Father wants. This means that if Jesus wills it, it will happen!

When you are ready to move on, say, **Sometimes we don't understand just what God's will is, but we should certainly seek to know and follow it.**

Option 1 (Little Prep)

Pray for specific needs.

Say, **Not only can we be recipients of God's compassion and love but we can be his agents of grace.** As we have been healed or blessed by God, we, too, can be instrumental in providing care to others. St. Francis of Assisi prayed this way:

Finish Line

> **Lord, make me an instrument of Your peace.**
> **Where there is hatred let me sow love;**
> **Where there is injury, pardon;**
> **Where there is doubt, faith;**
> **Where there is despair, hope;**
> **Where there is darkness, light;**
> **And where there is sadness, joy.**

Ask students to think specifically of people they could be instrumental in touching with the compassion of Christ this week. Close the session by praying that God will use your students to touch others at their point of need.

Note:

Don't forget to distribute copies of the Portable Sanctuary to students before they go.

Option 2 (More Prep)

Listen to a testimony and pray.

Invite someone who has experienced a healing in his or her life to visit and share the story with your class. This does not have to be limited to just a physical healing. If possible, you could invite multiple guests to share about different types of healing. Utilize any of the following questions with your guest, and encourage your students to ask their own:

- **What were you suffering from, and how were you healed?**
- **Did the healing come in the time and way you expected, or was it different? How so?**
- **In what other ways has God brought healing to your life?**

Explain that it's one thing to read a story about the touch of Christ—but quite another to experience or hear about this kind of compassion firsthand.

Close the session by praying for your guest and by asking God to use your students to touch others at their point of need.

Bible Charades

Genesis 3:6–8, 21

Jonah 4:5–6

Genesis 6:9–14

Matthew 17:24–27

Exodus 13:17–22

John 6:1–13

Joshua 6:1–20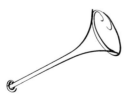

Acts 4:32–35

Leprosy Then and Now

Leprosy (also known as Hansen's disease) is characterized by skin lesions. If not treated, leprosy can be progressive, permanently damaging to the skin, nerves, limbs, and eyes. In 1995, it was estimated that up to three million people were permanently disabled because of leprosy. It is not known exactly how leprosy is transmitted, although prolonged close contact and transmission by inhalation are thought to be the most likely ways.

Large patches of leprosy may affect a whole limb, causing weakness and loss of sensation. The disease itself does not cause rotting of the flesh; due to damaged nerves, victims cannot feel wounds or lesions to the affected area, which allows undetected deterioration of the tissues.

In the 1940s, the drug *dapsone* was developed as a treatment for leprosy. Multidrug therapies developed in the early 1980s have provided even more effective treatments.

In the Bible, the original word used for *leprosy* could indicate various diseases affecting the skin. As you can imagine, the medical treatment available for leprosy (and many other diseases) was nonexistent at the time. Leprosy and any other visible skin disease were dealt with by isolating the people who had it. These people lived in colonies outside the main city; whenever someone came in proximity, the person with leprosy had to cry out, "Unclean! Unclean!" In Bible times, many people believed that sickness was a punishment from God for sin, thinking that people with leprosy were just "getting what was coming to them."

Portable Sanctuary

Day 1
Preparation, Part 1

Pastors don't stay at the same church forever; they either retire or go to another place of ministry at some point. Sometimes upon departing a pastor will say, "It's time for someone to take this congregation to the next level." When we serve God, we often build on the work of others who have come before us. As we submit to God's will, he will open the doors and lead us to the places he wants us to be. We can thank God for those who have prepared the way for us to serve.

Questions and Suggestions

- Read Mark 1:1–8. What was unique about John? How did he "prepare the way" for Jesus?
- Thank God for those who have prepared the way for you, and pray that you will be effective in preparing the way for others.

Day 2
Preparation, Part 2

Have you ever gotten a painful blister? This happens often to gymnasts and drummers, who grip repetitively with their hands. It can even happen if you do a lot of sweeping or raking. The top layer of skin gets loose and it hurts. Underneath, a new layer of skin is growing. When the old skin finally detaches completely and falls away, the new skin underneath is thicker and tougher. Experiencing temptation is never fun. But when we face it successfully, it makes us stronger for the future.

N O T E S

- Read Mark 1:9–13. How do you think the descending Spirit prepared Jesus for the upcoming temptation? How do you think the temptation prepared Jesus for ministry?

- If you're being tempted, seek God's help for the situation—and learn and grow from it.

Day 3
Preparation, Part 3

If you ever work in a job where you manage others, a key part of your strategy will be delegation. Delegation means assigning some tasks to other people who can effectively get them done. It doesn't mean you *can't* do the task—it means you find someone else who can, so that you can focus on other tasks. No one can do everything alone! Jesus knew this, so he invited others into ministry with him. He trained these people in what to do, then gave them the freedom to do it.

Questions and Suggestions

- Read Mark 1:14–20. How long did Simon, Andrew, James, and John have to consider Jesus' offer? What does this say about these men? What does it say about Jesus?

- Ask God to make you an effective member of the team, fulfilling your role in sharing his love.

Day 4
Sin and Healing

In Bible times, people often associated sickness with sin. If you were ill, or if something bad happened to you, it was thought to be punishment from God for something bad you had done. People would often beat themselves up trying to figure out how they had displeased God! Jesus turned this whole notion on its head. He knew that sin and sickness are often separate issues, but that sin is more important to deal with.

Whatever people looked like or said on the *outside*, Jesus knew what was going on on the *inside*.

Questions and Suggestions

- Read Mark 2:1–12. How determined were the friends of this man? Why? Do you need forgiveness or healing more in your own life? Why?

- God sees your heart. If you have issues, confess them to God. Deal with them and get them cleared up so you can be healed.

Day 5
Variety

One of the beautiful things about the church is its variety. God meets all sorts of people right where they are and calls them to follow him— male and female of every race, young and old, the rich and poor, the liberals and conservatives, and everything in between (when "between" can apply!). You are unique. God made you that way on purpose. Because of how you are and the things you have been through, you can touch some lives that other people will never reach.

Questions and Suggestions

- Read Mark 2:13–17. What is a place where you would be embarrassed, as a Christian, to be seen? Would you be tempted in this place, or could God use you there?

- Next time you're in church, look around at the diversity of people there and thank God for the beautiful mosaic he has created.

Leading into the Session

Warm Up

Option 1 Conduct a shoe discussion.
LITTLE PREP

Option 2 Make tuxedo shirts.
MORE PREP *White T-shirts, black permanent markers*

Starting Line

Option 1 Detect who is the leader.
YOUNGER YOUTH

Option 2 Identify "leader types."
OLDER YOUTH *Magazines*

Leading through the Session

Straight Away

Explore the Bible passage.
Bibles

The Turn

Discuss the struggle to serve.
Bibles, Reproducible 1, pens or pencils

Leading beyond the Session

Home Stretch

Option 1 Link good leading and good following.
YOUNGER YOUTH *Construction paper, scissors, poster board, tape*

Option 2 Rank leadership qualities.
OLDER YOUTH *Reproducible 2, pens or pencils*

Finish Line

Option 1 Share commitments to be servant leaders.
LITTLE PREP

Option 2 Serve as Jesus did.
MORE PREP *Pitchers of warm water, towels, basins; contemplative music (optional)*

SESSION 3

JESUS THE SERVANT

Bible Passage
John 13:1–17

Key Verse
Now that I, your Lord and Teacher, have washed your feet, you also should wash one another's feet.
—John 13:14

Main Thought
Jesus redefined leadership by serving.

Bible Background

The philosopher Aristotle reportedly observed that the virtue of patience is acquired not through reading books but by training horses. In other words, the virtues develop through use rather than by mastering information about them. Acquiring information is a form of cognitive learning, and the knowledge that comes through this form of learning is certainly important. Twenty-first century culture would be even more difficult to navigate without basic mathematical, reading, and technological information at our disposal. Many lessons lend themselves to lectures or even parables, but others require a different mode of instruction. Education for character has become a watchword in North American educational circles, but character develops in a learning environment that makes use of narrative *and* example.

The story of Jesus' washing his disciples' feet is a powerful moral lesson in humility and service. Jesus delivered no lecture. The disciples were not required to memorize a dictionary definition of humility or to perform a specified number of daily acts of service. Instead, Jesus removed his outer garment, took basin and water, and performed the most menial of tasks. In Semitic cultures the foot was an object of scorn and an instrument of insult. The westerner who carelessly crosses his or her legs in a crowd of Middle Easterners inadvertently insults anyone who sees the sole of his or her shoe. In ancient days only a servant would touch another person's feet, and only because washing them was his duty. Nevertheless, Jesus crossed this social barrier to wash the feet of his students.

The lesson was initially lost on Peter, quick to speak and yet so often slow to learn. Jesus had to interpret the little dramatic lesson that had just unfolded in the upper room. It is right to call Jesus Lord and Teacher, for so he is. But no disciple is greater than his or her teacher. Jesus' practical syllogism locked his followers into a service way of life: if disciples are not greater than the Master, and the Master washes feet, then his disciples must follow this example if they are to continue as his students.

Some Christians practice feet washing as one of three church ordinances. As an element of worship, feet washing is often a deeply moving experience for both the one washing and the one who receives it. However, it would be a serious interpretive mistake to think that Jesus' command is restricted to an act of worship. The command to wash one another's feet is also a metaphor for a servant attitude toward all our relationships. Thus Paul wrote, "Let this mind be in you which was also in Christ Jesus...." (Phil 2:5, KJV). The liturgical act of washing another's feet is good and proper, but its significance is outstripped by daily acts performed by those whose calling is based in service and who understand their vocation in Christian terms. Yet a life of service is not restricted to the caring professions; Jesus tells *all* of his disciples to wash somebody else's feet.

Warm Up

OPTION 1 (LITTLE PREP)
Conduct a shoe discussion.

As your students enter the room, ask them to remove their shoes and place them in a row. When everyone's shoes are off, discuss the following questions:

- **Could you easily identify which shoes belong to which person? Why or why not?**
- **Which shoes are the cleanest? dirtiest? smelliest? coolest?**
- **Would you be willing to put on any of these shoes besides your own? Why or why not?** We are often hesitant to wear someone else's shoes, as we consider feet to be dirty and the inside of shoes to be likewise disgusting.

Say, **Shoes—and feet—are not exactly the most popular things in the world.**

OPTION 2 (MORE PREP)
Make tuxedo shirts.

Bring to class enough white T-shirts for each student to have one, and some black permanent markers. (If you get the word out beforehand, you could have each student bring his or her own shirt.) Allow time for each student to create a shirt similar to the following:

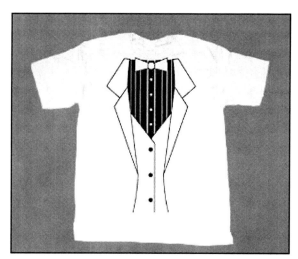

As your students are trying on their new shirts, ask, **What things do we usually associate with people who wear tuxedos?** Tuxedos are worn to fancy events and sometimes associated with rich people. Point out that they are also a standard uniform for some people who work as servants.

Say, **You look lovely in your new shirts! Are you ready to serve?**

> *Note:*
>
> If you will be doing FINISH LINE, Option 2 (More Prep), ask students to leave their shoes off.

> *Note:*
>
> If you sent the Portable Sanctuary home with students last week, take some time at the beginning of this session to review and discuss their experience.

Starting Line

OPTION 1 (YOUNGER YOUTH)

Detect who is the leader.

Select a volunteer to serve as "detective" and send this person out of the room. The rest of the group should sit in a circle and then choose a leader. Explain that everyone should follow what the leader does when the detective returns to the room.

Bring the detective back into the room and ask him or her to stand in the middle of the circle. The idea is for the leader to do various motions (subtle at first) that everyone else follows, without being identified by the "detective" as the leader. How long can the leader continue changing actions without being detected by the detective? If there is time after the leader is caught, you can play another round in which he or she becomes the detective.

When the game is through, ask the detective(s), **How did you figure out who the leader really was?** The students had to look at the leader for direction; eventually the detective picked up on this. Point out that leaders are the first ones to do a certain thing. They stand out in the sense that their actions are more obvious.

When you are ready to move on, say, **Let's look at a story that shows just what kind of a leader Jesus was.**

· ·

OPTION 2 (OLDER YOUTH)

Identify "leader types."

Furnish a variety of magazines *(Time, Newsweek, People, Seventeen, Sports Illustrated,* and so forth) and give the students time to comb through the magazines, looking for pictures of people who would likely be considered leaders. These may be people the students recognize, or people who just strike your students as "leader types."

After a few minutes, ask the students to share the pictures they have selected and explain why they chose those people as leaders. Point out that appearance has a lot to do with our impression of people as leaders—we usually expect that leaders will be good looking, or perhaps look "smart." In reality, looks have very little to do with whether or not someone is a good leader.

When you are ready to move on, say, **Let's look at a story that shows just what kind of a leader Jesus was.**

Leading through the Session

Straight Away

Explore the Bible passage.

Read together John 13:1–17 and discuss the following questions:

• **Washing feet was commonly done by the household servant as soon as guests arrived. Why do you think the disciples' feet had not already been washed?** Perhaps they had been and the text does not mention it; perhaps there was no servant present to do the task; or perhaps Jesus instructed the servant to leave the task for Jesus to do. Regardless the reason or the circumstances, Jesus took on the role of servant when he washed his disciples' feet.

- **Why do you think Jesus sensed that this was a good time to show his disciples "the full extent of his love"?** He knew that he would be crucified soon and then be leaving his friends. These would be shocking events for them. When we are facing a separation, it's a good time to let our loved ones know how we feel about them.
- **What is significant about the fact that Judas had already been prompted to betray Jesus?** Jesus knew that this man would start a chain of events that would end his life, yet he still chose to wash his feet. What an incredible example of love and servanthood.
- **In what order did Jesus put teaching and action here?** Jesus began with action; he got up without explanation and washed the disciples' feet. When they had questions he answered them. When the act was done, he explained why he had done it and what it meant for the disciples in the future.
- **What was Peter's argument to the whole thing—and how did Jesus respond?** Peter seemed to feel that Jesus was "above" doing such a task. Jesus linked the act of footwashing and participation in his mission. Peter argued with Jesus (perhaps a little sarcastically), and Jesus clarified that the act of footwashing was in response to a specific need.
- **How did this footwashing show the disciples the "full extent" of Jesus' love for them?** If any of your students have ever participated in a footwashing service, they know that it's a very personal and touching experience. Regardless of the culture we live in, to be kneeling before someone and washing his or her feet is a humbling, intimate act. The disciples had seen Jesus do some pretty amazing things, but now he showed them that serving them was very important to him.
- **If Jesus served others and washed their feet, how important is it for *us* to do so?** Jesus pointed out that the servant is not greater than the master. If he did this for us, then we are even more obligated to do it for one another.
- **How are there "layers" to Jesus' command for us to follow his example and wash one another's feet?** Basically, we should literally wash one another's feet. Beyond this, we should take the most humble role and serve one another sacrificially. That's what leaders in the kingdom of God do.

Say, **Jesus redefined leadership in the eyes of his disciples.**

Discuss the struggle to serve.

Distribute copies of "The Struggle to Serve" (Reproducible 1) or show it as a projection. The students should look up the passages given and answer the associated questions. (You can have class members work on this individually, in pairs or small groups, or all together.) Discuss responses; here are some suggestions:

The Turn

- Matthew 20:20–28—James and John's mother asked Jesus to give her sons the positions of honor in his kingdom. Jesus told them that it was not up to him, and that they should follow the model of servanthood he had set. In the kingdom of God our goal should be to serve others, not to pursue a particular title or position.
- Luke 9:46–56—The disciples were arguing about which of them was greatest. Jesus used a child to show that those who welcome children—and are humble as children—are greatest in God's kingdom. The disciples also

tried to "punish" people who were ministering in other groups or who did not receive Jesus' message, but Jesus told them not to. In God's kingdom, leadership is about humility and service—not about power.

- Luke 22:24–27—The disciples were arguing about which of them was greatest. Jesus said that those who are greatest should serve, just as he did. In God's kingdom, leadership is not about a title or position—it's about service.

Point out that the Bible presents a very honest picture of the struggles and failures of God's people. In each of these instances the disciples struggled to understand their roles as followers of Christ and leaders of others. Jesus was patient with them and continued to teach them what true leadership is all about.

Say, **Jesus showed that we lead by putting others' needs first, providing for people's needs, and being humble.**

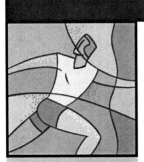

Home Stretch

OPTION 1 (YOUNGER YOUTH)
Link good leading and good following.

Bring to class various colors of construction paper. Using the paper, cut two identical sets of geometric shapes. (Tip: Fold each sheet of paper in half and cut both sets at the same time.) Each set should contain the following:

- 3 squares of different sizes and/or colors
- 2 triangles of different sizes and/or colors
- 1 circle

Choose two volunteers. Tell the group that the shorter person will be the leader and the taller person will be the follower. Give one set of shapes, a piece of poster board, and a roll of tape to each volunteer, then ask the follower to exit the room. Ask the leader to take the set of geometric shapes and tape them to the poster board in any way he or she likes. Allow the group to watch as the leader does this. Bring the follower back into the room, and make sure the leader is positioned so the follower cannot see the shapes on the poster board. Now, ask the leader to explain to the follower, using only verbal communication, how to arrange the shapes to match the leader's. The leader cannot show his or her poster board, and the leader cannot look at the follower's poster board. The follower may ask questions.

After the follower is done, display the two poster boards side by side and discuss the following questions:

- **How are the posters alike? How are they different? Why?**
- *To the leader*—**What was it like to give instructions but not know how they were being followed?**
- *To the follower*—**What was it like to receive instructions but no feedback on how you were actually doing?**
- **How could these two volunteers have communicated more effectively?**
  The most effective leadership involves close communication between the

leader and the followers, an ongoing dialogue about what is happening and the ability for the follower to observe what the leader is doing along the way.

When you are ready to move on, say, **Effective leaders work closely and openly with those they are teaching and serving.**

OPTION 2 (OLDER YOUTH)

Rank leadership qualities.

Distribute copies of "Leadership Qualities" (Reproducible 2), go over the instructions, and allow time for students to complete the handout. After a few minutes, discuss which qualities students ranked as most important, and why they chose as they did. Discuss how we often choose leaders without giving serious consideration to the qualities that are really important. Point out that Jesus did more than give us a good example of servant leadership; he left behind instructions that we should do the same.

When you are ready to move on, say, **Jesus didn't promise that serving would be fun, glamorous, or successful. He just said, "I did it—you do it too."**

OPTION 1 (LITTLE PREP)

Share commitments to be servant leaders.

Say, **Christians are supposed to be followers or imitators of Christ. That's what our name means! When was the last time you served someone?** Share about a recent time when you might have missed such an opportunity. Suggest to the students some of the projects and ministries in which your congregation participates. Point out that God wants to give us the heart of a servant, just like Jesus had when he washed the disciples' feet. We can lead as Jesus led by serving others.

End the session by praying together. You may want to invite the students to raise their hands or in some way indicate their desire to more closely follow Christ's example of leadership.

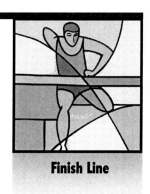

Finish Line

Note:

Don't forget to distribute copies of the Portable Sanctuary to students before they go.

OPTION 2 (MORE PREP)

Serve as Jesus did.

Provide pitchers of warm water, towels, and basins. Ask your students to remove their shoes and socks. (While you want to encourage participation by everyone, give those who do not wish to take part the option of observing.) Demonstrate how to proceed by pouring water into one of the basins so that the basin is roughly one-third full. Then take the basin and a towel and go to a same-gender student. Place one of the individual's feet in the basin, wash it, and dry it. Do the same with the other foot. As you are performing this symbolic act of servanthood, you might want to tell that person something you appreciate about him or her. You may even want to give that individual a hug after you are finished. Then dump the used water into an empty basin or sink and set the towel aside.

Invite students to begin washing one another's feet. If possible, students should wash the feet of same-gender learners. (This will cut down on embarrassment that could detract from the significance of the moment.) While all of this is taking place, you may want to play some contemplative music in the background.

When students have washed someone's feet, advise them to be seated and wait for someone to come to them. Be sure that everyone has both washed someone's feet and has had his or her own feet washed before you complete this activity.

Explain that Jesus modeled servanthood for us. You have just participated in a highly significant, symbolic act of servanthood. Though there may have been some embarrassment associated with it, your group members have just followed the example Jesus gave. Discuss how it felt to wash someone else's feet, and to have someone else wash your own feet. Point out that God wants to give us the heart of a servant, just like Jesus had when he washed the disciples' feet. We can lead as Jesus led by serving others.

End the session by praying together. You may want to invite the students to raise their hands or in some way indicate a desire to more closely follow Christ's example of leadership.

The Struggle to Serve

Jesus gave the disciples a new model of leadership, but they struggled to understand what it meant. Read each passage below to see what the disciples did and what Jesus taught them.

Matthew 20:20–28

What did the disciples do? Why do you think they responded this way?_____
_____
_____

How did Jesus respond to the disciples? _____
_____
_____

What does this teach us about leadership in the kingdom of God? _____
_____
_____

Luke 9:46–56

What did the disciples do? Why do you think they responded this way?_____
_____
_____

How did Jesus respond to the disciples? _____
_____
_____

What does this teach us about leadership in the kingdom of God? _____
_____
_____

Luke 22:24–26

What did the disciples do? Why do you think they responded this way?_____
_____
_____

How did Jesus respond to the disciples? _____
_____

What does this teach us about leadership in the kingdom of God? _____
_____
_____

Leadership Qualities

In your opinion, which of the following qualities are most important for a leader to possess? Rank them from 1 on down, with 1 being the most important. There are blanks to add some other qualities you may think of.

Rank   **Leaders should be...**

_____   willing to try anything once.

_____   intelligent.

_____   goal-oriented.

_____   flexible.

_____   accepting of different ideas and opinions.

_____   unselfish.

_____   self-motivated.

_____   imaginative.

_____   honest and not deceptive.

_____   practical and resourceful.

_____   _____

_____   _____

Now go back to the list of qualities. Check all of the qualities that you possess. Be honest—you don't have to share this with the rest of the group.

Portable Sanctuary

Day 1
A Leader by Birth

Monarchies (rule by kings and queens) are somewhat foreign to us in North America today. After all, we elect our leaders at all levels of government. A ruler's son or daughter is not guaranteed to be a leader; such a person must run on his or her own merits. If you are expected to be a leader like your mother or father, the pressure placed upon you is great (just look at all the turmoil that England's royal family has been through!). Some people seem destined from birth to be leaders.

Questions and Suggestions

- Read Exodus 2:1–10. How was God looking out for Moses' future? How did Moses' discovery by Pharaoh's daughter prepare him for future leadership?
- When you were a kid, were you a leader or a follower in school? Remember, Jesus taught *all* of us to lead by serving others.

Day 2
A Leader Runs

Exile means to be banished from one's people or country. This can be forced on a person by others or it can be voluntary. When political leaders get into trouble, sometimes they go into exile in another country. (This happens more often in Africa and South America than in North America.) These leaders flee their own country because if they return, they will be imprisoned or murdered. Returning from exile before all is well can be a very risky proposition.

- Read Exodus 2:11–15. Do you think Moses was wrong in defending his fellow countryman? What might have happened if he had not fled?
- Sometimes God uses times of exile or loneliness to prepare us. Ask God to use your current circumstances to prepare you for greater things.

Day 3
The Call of Leadership

Those who have followed God's call into ministry will tell you that the call was a powerful one. God doesn't usually speak to us in an audible voice, but he does speak to our hearts. Some people flee from the call and try to busy themselves with other careers, but they're not happy until they do what God has asked. God calls people into all kinds of service, not just as full-time pastors or missionaries. If God is speaking to you, answer him. Seek guidance from other trusted Christians. And follow the call.

Questions and Suggestions

- Read Exodus 3:1–10. Why do you think God chose to speak through a burning bush? How did Moses approach God? How should we?
- Keep your eyes open for ways that God might be speaking to you.

Day 4
Twisting and Squirming

Have you ever talked to someone who won't take no for an answer? Such a person might ask something of you, and you really don't want to do it, so you say no. This person doesn't buy the reason you give, so he or she gives some reasons why should do it. You start to think of more reasons why you shouldn't do it. If you know in your heart that you should do it, you start to get a little uncomfortable—twisting and squirming. If you finally listen to your conscience, you change your answer to yes.

Questions and Suggestions

- Read Exodus 3:11–14. How did God try to soothe Moses' fears? What is significant about God calling himself "I AM"?
- Search your heart for anything God is asking you to do that you have been resisting. Pray about it.

Day 5
Leadership Credentials

There is a certain amount of respect that goes along with a leadership position. To an extent, people will respect you just because you're in leadership. But beyond that, respect must be earned. People dig up past history on new leaders to see whether or not these leaders are worthy of respect. When leaders are caught in lies or make bad decisions, people quickly lose trust in them. They stop following—and when the next election occurs, these leaders are voted out of office.

Questions and Suggestions

- Read Exodus 4:1–9. How would you respond to seeing a transforming staff, instant leprosy, and a river turned to blood?
- These unique signs were given to show that God was with Moses. Pray that others will see something different in your life—something to show that God is with you too.

Leading into the Session

Warm Up

Option 1 Play Guess Who?
LITTLE PREP *Blindfold*

Option 2 Play a name game.
MORE PREP *Reproducible 1 (prepared beforehand), pens or pencils*

Starting Line

Option 1 Identify people.
YOUNGER YOUTH *Baby pictures of students*

Option 2 Predict your death.
OLDER YOUTH *Paper, pens or pencils; chalkboard or dry erase board (optional)*

Leading through the Session

Straight Away

Explore the Bible passage.
Bibles

The Turn

Examine the incredible claims of Christ.
Chalkboard or dry erase board (optional)

Leading beyond the Session

Home Stretch

Option 1 Identify the pros and cons of knowing
YOUNGER YOUTH **Christ.**
Reproducible 2, pens or pencils

Option 2 Conduct a pretend interview.
OLDER YOUTH *Someone to dress up like Jesus (optional)*

Finish Line

Option 1 Discuss practical ways to discover Jesus.
LITTLE PREP *Chalkboard or dry erase board*

Option 2 Assign some "Gospel homework."
MORE PREP *Time outside of class; Bible resources such as Bible dictionaries and commentaries*

SESSION 4

JESUS THE CONQUEROR

Bible Passage
Matthew 16:13–23

Key Verse
On this rock I will build my church, and the gates of Hades will not overcome it.
—Matthew 16:18

Main Thought
Jesus has conquered hell—and what he establishes cannot be overcome.

The interpretation of Matthew 16:13ff creates one of the great divides that separates Christians from one another. On one side of the divide is the Roman Catholic church and an interpretation that serves as the foundation of the papacy. It should be noted that Roman Christians early on called their bishop "Papa," from which comes the word *pope*. However, centuries passed before the institution of the papacy acquired the authority and prestige associated with modern-day popes. In fact, it was not until the first Vatican Council in 1870 that the idea of the infallibility of the pope was made Catholic dogma. Much earlier, two popes, Leo I in the fifth century and Gregory I in the sixth, contributed enormously to the stature of the papacy by their actions, orthodoxy, and instruction. Around them and the papacy there grew the interpretive tradition that Jesus' declaration, "You are Peter, and on this rock I will build my church," gave Peter and his successor bishops of Rome the keys of the kingdom and authority to lead the whole body of believers.

Protestants of course dispute this interpretation. Much Protestant ink has been spilled over two forms of the word *rock* in the Greek New Testament. Jesus said to Simon, "You are *Petros* and upon this *petra* I will build my church." Those who use this grammatical point to build a theological objection to Catholic teaching should be reminded that Jesus spoke to Peter in Aramaic, not Greek, and Aramaic has but one form of the word *rock*, *kepha*, which some versions transliterate as "Cephas." Protestants, however, can find allies among some early Christian interpreters of the Bible. Theodore of Mopsuestia founded a literalist school of interpretation at Antioch and was a younger contemporary of Pope Leo I. About this text Theodore wrote, "This is not the property of Peter alone, but it came about on behalf of every human being. Having said that his confession is a rock, he [Jesus] stated that upon this rock I will build my church. This means he will build his church upon this same confession and faith [that Jesus is the Christ, the Son of the living God]. On account of Peter's confession he applied to him this authority, too, as something that would become his, speaking of the common and special good of the church.... By this he shows ... the common element of the confession was to come to be first in Peter."[1]

Almost lost in the interpretive debate is Jesus' question, one that confronts all who have heard the gospel: "Who do you say that I am?" The question is not "What?" but "Who?" It will not do to answer with an analysis. The only acceptable answer entails a decision whether one will be his disciple; Christian discipleship is, first and foremost, loyalty to Jesus—God's Messiah.

1. Manlio Simonetti, ed., *Matthew,* from the series Ancient Christian Commentary on Scripture: New Testament, Vol. Ib (Downers Grove: InterVarsity Press, 2002), 45–46.

OPTION 1 (LITTLE PREP)

Play Guess Who?

Pick a volunteer and ask this person to take a minute to become acquainted with everyone else's elbows. Blindfold the volunteer, mix up the other students, and see if your volunteer can correctly identify, by touch, whom the different elbows belong to. After the game is through, ask, **How much evidence does it take to convince you of a person's identity?** Instead of touch, we usually use sight and sound to identify someone. The more familiar we are with someone, the easier that person is to identify by just a glance or a brief word.

Say, **Being able to identify people makes relationships possible.**

Warm Up

. . . .

OPTION 2 (MORE PREP)

Play a name game.

Place the names of your students in "Name Game" (Reproducible 1) according to the instructions given there. Distribute copies to your students and see how they do at finding the names in this customized word search. You can throw extra names in for fun, but don't give an exact list of names to the class; let them see what they can find. Afterwards, point out that it's easier to identify a person when we know him or her. In this case it would have been easier—particularly for someone new to your class—to identify the names to find if someone had spelled out the exact names to look for.

Say, **The better we know someone, the better relationship we can have with that person.**

Note:

If you sent the Portable Sanctuary home with students last week, take some time at the beginning of this session to review and discuss their experience.

OPTION 1 (YOUNGER YOUTH)

Identify people.

Collect baby pictures of your students and make a display of them (without names). Invite students to try to guess who is who. (You can either ask students to bring the pictures beforehand or else contact their parents and collect the pictures secretly.) Do any students seem to have a knack for identifying old pictures like this? Did any students fail to recognize even their own pictures? Ask, **How could someone identify you from a baby picture like this?** We all have physical traits (hair and eye color, smile, face shape, and so forth) that tend to last over time. If we can pick up on some of these traits, we can figure out what a person used to (or will) look like.

When you are ready to move on, say, **Let's see what Peter and the disciples came to understand about Jesus' identity.**

Starting Line

OPTION 2 (OLDER YOUTH)

Predict your death.

Distribute paper and pens or pencils to the students and invite them to write down answers to the following questions (you may wish to write them on the board):

- **How old do you think you'll live to be?**
- **If you could choose the way you will die, what way would you choose and why?**
- **What might be a *possible* death for you based on any hobbies or activities (particularly dangerous ones such as bungee jumping or skydiving) that you enjoy or would like to try?**

After the students have written their responses, discuss their thoughts.

When you are ready to move on, say, **It would be kind of creepy if we could accurately predict our own death. Let's see how Jesus actually did this.**

Leading through the Session

Straight Away

Explore the Bible passage.

Read together Matthew 16:13–23 and discuss the following questions:

- **Who did people think Jesus was—and why would they think this?** Some said John the Baptist, some said Elijah, and others said Jeremiah or one of the prophets. Because of his teaching and miracles, many people definitely thought that Jesus was from God. John had ministered just before Jesus, so there was a connection there. Elijah had done some miracles as Jesus did.
- **Do you think Jesus really didn't know what people were saying about him? If he did know, why would he ask his disciples?** The contrast was made clear between what the public thought and what Peter and Jesus' closest followers thought. The disciples didn't fully understand Jesus' mission until after his resurrection, but they gave evidence here that they were growing in their understanding.
- **How do people in our world today mistake Jesus' identity?** Some say he was only a good teacher. Some say that it's too simple or narrow for Jesus to be the only way to heaven. Some people see Christians who don't act much like Jesus, so they think there must not be any real substance to Jesus.
- **How do you think Peter knew that Jesus was "the Christ, the Son of the living God"?** He had been with Jesus for many miracles, healings, and powerful teaching. Jesus was certainly unique, and Peter had never known anyone like him before. Jesus said it was God who had revealed Jesus' identity to Peter. Point out that God speaks to all human beings by his grace; it's up to us to listen and respond.
- **What was significant about the new name Jesus gave Peter?** *Peter* means "rock." Peter had just demonstrated a strong, solid faith in Jesus Christ as the Son of God. Such a faith is so strong that even hell itself ("Hades") can't destroy it!
- **What did Jesus mean by all this "binding" and "loosing"?** Christ's

followers follow his will and operate in his power. When we truly act in the name of Christ, heaven is behind us—whether we are "binding" something (restricting it or coming against it) or "loosing" something (supporting it or setting it free).

- **How did Peter respond when Jesus spelled out the future suffering, death, and resurrection that would occur? Why?** He rebuked Jesus (basically told him he was wrong). Peter loved Jesus and would definitely not want to see him suffer and die. In Peter's mind, suffering and death were not the kinds of things that would happen to the Son of God!
- **Jesus got pretty harsh with Peter! What is a "stumbling block," and how was Peter acting like one?** This term means just what it sounds like—something to make a person trip and fall. Jesus' mission was the cross, but Peter was determined that Jesus would not suffer in that way. Even Jesus had to submit his own will to God in order to face the cross (see Luke 22:39–44). Denying the Crucifixion was denying the plan of God to offer salvation to all.

Say, **Jesus knew that a solid faith in him was more powerful than even hell itself.**

The Turn

Examine the incredible claims of Christ.

Think of some statements or claims Jesus made about himself and invite the students to consider what they might mean for us today. Here are some possibilities; feel free to add others (you may wish to write them on the board):

- *Jesus is the Bread of Life.*
- *Jesus is the Living Water.*
- *Jesus is the Good Shepherd.*
- *Jesus is the Light of the World.*
- *Jesus is the Way.*
- *Jesus is the Truth.*
- *Jesus is the Life.*

You can divide the class into pairs or small groups, or discuss together these claims. Explain that by using such language, Jesus helped his disciples—and us—to understand better who he is and why he came. He used figurative language to concretely express difficult abstract ideas. You might ask, **What is the purpose of bread, of water, of a shepherd? How are these things used or needed in our world? What does our world substitute for these items?** For example, Jesus didn't say, "I am the Coca-Cola of the world"; he said that he is the living water because we all need water to survive and be healthy. People substitute things such as sodas, coffee, and alcohol for what they really need—water. Spiritually, people substitute things for Jesus. These things can include being popular, making good grades, excelling at something, having money, being good, and so forth.

When you are ready to move on, say, **When Christ says something is true, we can take it as fact.**

Home Stretch

OPTION 1 (YOUNGER YOUTH)

Identify the pros and cons of knowing Christ.

Distribute copies of "Getting to Know You" (Reproducible 2), go over the instructions, and allow the students time to complete the handout. After a few minutes, ask class members to pair up, compare their charts, and combine their thoughts onto one of the papers. After a couple of minutes, combine the pairs with other pairs and have them combine thoughts again. Do this as many times as time or class size allows, then invite the final groups to share their thoughts with the rest of the class. Ask, **Did anyone make any statements that you think are untrue? Which side outweighs the other, the pros or the cons?** Point out that while it may sound strange to admit, there seems to be a "benefit" to not knowing Jesus. It's kind of like knowing that you're sick and not going to the doctor because you don't want to hear the bad news. You might feel as if you are happier in your ignorance, but if you had gone to the doctor when you first got sick, the problem might not have become so severe. It's the same with Jesus; if we would admit we need him and that our lives are a mess, we could avoid many mistakes and hurts. Inviting Jesus in, however, also means that we need to do what he says. We don't always think that God's way is best. If you go to the doctor and don't follow his plan, you stay sick. If you go to Jesus and don't follow *his* plan, you stay spiritually sick and feel guilty.

When you are ready to move on, say, **"Knowing" Christ means more than knowing *about* Christ; it means seeking a relationship with him and surrendering to his guidance.**

. . . .

OPTION 2 (OLDER YOUTH)

Conduct a pretend interview.

If possible, arrange for someone your students do not know to visit the class dressed as Jesus. If a guest is not possible, you can play the role yourself. Even the costume is optional if you explain to the students what you are doing. Say, **Pretend that Jesus is actually here with us, in the flesh, right now. What would you like to say to him or ask him?** Encourage creativity and a significant amount of seriousness in the midst of the "funny" questions. Your guest (or you) should attempt to answer as Jesus would. After each question is answered, ask, **Would you *really* ask Jesus this?**

When you are ready to move on, say, **Knowing Jesus better will change the kinds of questions we ask him.**

Option 1 (Little Prep)

Discuss practical ways to discover Jesus.

Ask your students to brainstorm different practical ways that people can discover who Jesus is and the difference he can make in their lives. As the students share their ideas, list them on the board. Here are some possibilities:

Finish Line

- Read the Bible on a regular basis.
- Join a Bible study.
- Ask a Christ-follower about his or her relationship with Jesus.
- Watch the *Jesus* movie.
- Read about someone who did a lot for God.
- Keep a prayer journal to see how God faithfully answers prayer.
- Take notes during the Sunday morning message.
- Listen to Christian music.
- Spend time in prayer each day.

Close the session in prayer, challenging the students to choose one or two of the suggestions to implement in their journey to know Jesus better.

Note:

Don't forget to distribute copies of the Portable Sanctuary to students before they go.

· ·

Option 2 (More Prep)

Assign some "Gospel homework."

If think your students are up for the commitment of a challenge, assign them to each choose one of the four Gospels (Matthew, Mark, Luke, or John) to do some independent study on. Furnish Bible resources such as Bible dictionaries and commentaries for students to use in their homework; you might also direct them to Web sites you have found useful. Make appointments to meet with students individually to encourage their work and help answer any questions they may have. Say, **One of the best ways to know Jesus better is to spend some time in one of the stories that tells us about his life.**

Close the session in prayer, asking God to reveal Jesus Christ more fully to your students as they seek to know him better.

Name Game

Place the names of your students in the grid below to create a personalized crossword puzzle for your class. Depending on the number of students you have, you can include last names too. You can use a bigger grid if necessary, or a computer to construct your own. Fill in the rest of the grid with random letters. Cut out the grid and instructions, make copies, and distribute to the students.

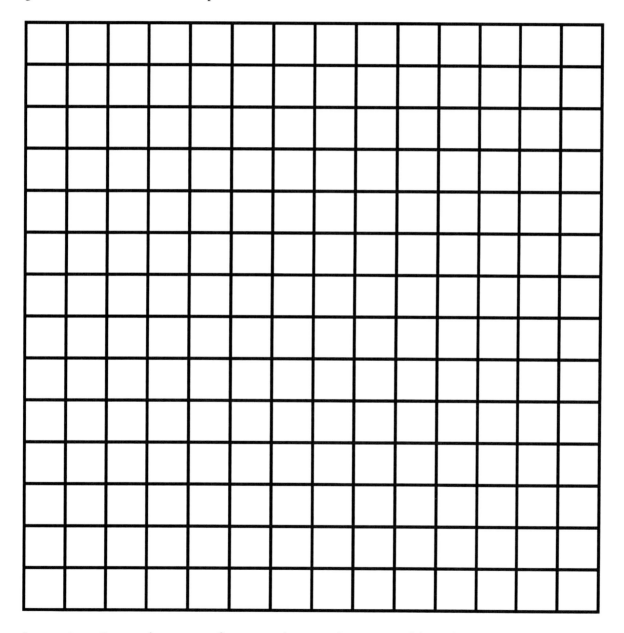

Instructions: Locate the names of as many class members as possible in this puzzle, according to the directions your leader gives.

Getting to Know You

Think about reasons why persons do not want to know Christ and reasons why persons do want to know Christ. List some reasons on this decision-making chart:

Pros
Yes to Christ

Why would I want to know Christ?
Is it worth it?

Cons
No to Christ

_____

_____

_____

_____

_____

_____

_____

_____

_____

_____

_____

_____

_____

_____

Look at the pros and cons listed above. Which side outweighs the other? What do you think?

Portable Sanctuary

Day 1

The Bread of Life

Bread has been around for a long time, and it's a basic food staple for many people. There are many types of bread, and many ways to prepare it. Even if you're not a very good cook, you can probably successfully make toast! Bread fills the stomach and satisfies the appetite. Jesus offered bread that satisfies forever; those who eat it will never be hungry again. Over the centuries, millions of people have found this source of eternal life and begun to enjoy the meal!

Questions and Suggestions

• Read John 6:35–40. What source does "Jesus the bread" have that enables him to eternally satisfy?

• If you're spiritually hungry, ask the Bread of Life to fill you.

Day 2

The Living Water

When water is flowing, it almost seems to be alive. Water itself contains life. Even if you drink purified or bottled water, there is still life in it—microorganisms that are harmless to you and go unnoticed by you. Water is also necessary to sustain life. You can probably survive for weeks without food, but not long at all without water! Jesus offered water that quenches the deepest thirst of our souls. He promised that those who drink of this water will never thirst again.

N O T E S

- Read John 4:1–14. What was unusual about Jesus speaking with this person?
- Read beyond verse 14 to see how this simple encounter changed a whole town. If you're spiritually thirsty, ask the Living Water to fill your soul.

Day 3
The Good Shepherd

Sheep are totally dependent on the shepherd. The shepherd leads them to good sources of food and water. Sheep do not have any natural defense mechanisms such as speed, sharp teeth, or pointy horns; the shepherd protects them from being attacked by predators. Good shepherds know each of their sheep and truly care about them. Jesus called himself *the* good shepherd. Not only does he provide nourishment for our souls, he also protects them from harm.

Questions and Suggestions

- Read John 10:11–18. How has Jesus "laid down his life" for the sheep? How does he know us? What "other sheep" does he have?
- Thank God for the peace that comes from knowing that the Good Shepherd is watching over you.

Day 4
The Light of the World

Light provides warmth, keeping us alive. It also allows us to see. Even the smallest amount of light can brighten a dark room. The sun is an enormous light; millions of earths could fit inside of it! Even though the earth is millions of miles from the sun, the sun provides all the warmth we need. Sometimes we get too much of the sun's light—and end up with a nasty sunburn! Jesus said that he is the light of the world—an eternal life that banishes the darkness forever.

- Read John 8:12–18. In what areas of your life has Jesus brought light and warmth? Where does Jesus get his light?
- If you're cold or stumbling around in the dark, ask Jesus to come in and light up your life.

Day 5
The Way, the Truth, and the Life

How many ways are there to get to your house? If you live on a dead end street, there may be just one road, but you could also climb over the back fence to get there. You could parachute in, too. What is truth? Two plus two is four, no matter how you look at it. How many lives do we have? Just one. Once you die, you begin living the rest of your life. There are no second chances. Jesus said that he is the way, the truth, and the life. That's about as specific as you can get!

Questions and Suggestions

- Read John 14:5–7. What is so "exclusive" about this claim? Why do some people resist or reject it?
- Thank Jesus for making a way for you. Seek to grow in your understanding of his truth. And take every chance to share his life with others.

CHRIST IN US

Note:

There is a teaching commentary on the Book of James available on the Digital BRIDGES CD.

When Jesus Christ becomes our Lord and Savior we are new creations. We begin to be challenged to live and act in new ways that are glorifying to God. This new way is not always easy. It contradicts what we are used to. We continually have to make a conscious effort to follow in the way of Christ. The Epistle of James provides believers with many words of wisdom regarding how to live as followers of Jesus.

Session 1 will explore the importance of living out our faith and not just talking about it. Session 2 will consider how we should treat all people equally and not show favoritism. Session 3 will help students understand the importance of using speech wisely. Session 4 will discuss the necessity of submitting our lives to God. Session 5 will encourage students to develop a life of prayer.

James is a book of action. What a great study for a youth group!

Unit 3 Special Prep

SESSION 1—WARM UP, Option 2 (More Prep), requires a tray, a towel, and various common household items. FINISH LINE, Option 2 (More Prep), calls for the time, transportation, and permission to take your group off-site to minister.

SESSION 2—WARM UP, Option 2 (More Prep), requires snack foods that have had their color altered with food coloring. HOME STRETCH, Option 1 (Younger Youth), calls for inexpensive rings that can be written on, and fine-point markers. FINISH LINE, Option 2 (More Prep), requires Band-Aids and fine-point markers.

SESSION 3—For WARM UP, Option 1 (Little Prep), you can use candy or other small prizes. Option 2 (More Prep) calls for Starburst-type candies, cherries, and small straws. STARTING LINE, Option 1 (Younger Youth), requires a dog trainer or animal trainer with a subject in training; you can also use the Digital BRIDGES CD, a computer, and a data projector. HOME STRETCH, Option 1 (Younger Youth), calls for thank-you cards. FINISH LINE, Option 2 (More Prep), requires various colors of thread and beads, and scissors.

SESSION 4—WARM UP, Option 1 (Little Prep), calls for duct tape. Option 2 (More Prep) requires a messy item to serve as "bacon," cleaning supplies, and candy or other small prizes. STARTING LINE, Option 1 (Younger Youth), calls for premade signs, paper strips, tape, and a marker. For Option 2 (Older Youth) you can use a green robe, hat, and/or face paint, and wet wipes. For HOME STRETCH, Option 1 (Younger Youth), you can use background worship music. Option 2 (Older Youth) requires a pitcher of water, a bowl, and towels; you can also use background worship music. FINISH LINE, Option 2 (More Prep), calls for helium balloons on strings and permanent markers.

SESSION 5—WARM UP, Option 2 (More Prep), requires *Happy, Sad, Angry,* and *Concerned/ Fearful* signs and accompanying decorations. STARTING LINE, Option 1 (Younger Youth), calls for large cutout letters *P-R-A-Y-E-R.* Option 2 (Older Youth) requires copies of different types of prayers, and tape. FINISH LINE, Option 2 (More Prep), calls for the time, transportation, and arrangements necessary to attend a prayer or healing service.

Leading into the Session

Warm Up

Option 1 — LITTLE PREP — Participate in an observation activity.
Reproducible 1, paper, pens or pencils

Option 2 — MORE PREP — Play a memory game.
Tray, towel, paper, pens or pencils, various common household items

Starting Line

Option 1 — YOUNGER YOUTH — Dramatize a parable.
Bibles

Option 2 — OLDER YOUTH — Discuss things we know but do not apply.
Chalkboard or dry erase board

Leading through the Session

Straight Away

Explore the Bible passage.
Bibles, chalkboard or dry erase board, Reproducible 2, pens or pencils

The Turn

Discuss the need to obey God's Word.
Bibles

Leading beyond the Session

Home Stretch

Option 1 — YOUNGER YOUTH — Confess personal hardships to one another.

Option 2 — OLDER YOUTH — Determine areas of needed growth.
Reproducible 2, pens or pencils

Finish Line

Option 1 — LITTLE PREP — Discuss faithful responses.

Option 2 — MORE PREP — Plan and implement a ministry trip.
Time, transportation, and permission to take your group off-site

The famed reformer Martin Luther distinguished between the word of Scripture and the Word of the gospel. He respected the entire canonical Scriptures, but he also considered some of their contents more important than others. Scripture, said Luther, is the cradle in which lays Christ the Word. The Word of Christ, that is to say, the gospel, was for Luther the core of the Bible. In his eyes this did not necessarily relegate the Old Testament to secondary status. Luther could also find the gospel there; for example, he read Psalm 19 as a prophetic description of Christ. By the same token he did not value equally the entire canon of the New Testament. Thus Luther famously declared the Letter of James to be a "book of straw" because it contained little or none of the gospel of justification by faith. Much to Luther's dislike, the theme of James is good works, which Luther consistently suspected of tempting believers away from God's grace and relying instead on their achievements to gain God's favor.

Protestants were already in sharp disagreement before Luther's death in the 1540s. Shortly afterward the situation degenerated into hotly contested polemics and even wars in the name of religion. In this highly charged atmosphere all parties tended to emphasize their theological distinctiveness. In the case of Lutherans that led to an extreme emphasis on justification by faith. Seventeenth-century Lutheran catechisms went so far as to discourage people from pursuing good works lest they become a source of self-righteousness. In reaction to this doctrinal extremism a German Lutheran pastor named Johann Arndt published a book called *True Christianity* in which he insisted on an experiential faith that showed itself to be true by producing good works: the roots of a man or woman's faith were to bear fruit in the conduct of their lives. Arndt's book was the fountainhead of a German Lutheran renewal movement called Pietism. Pietists certainly thought that the Bible was to be believed and the source of Christian teaching; even more they insisted that it is a book to be lived, emphasizing a very practical approach to Christian life. Pietists, in other words, did not share the historic Lutheran antipathy for the Letter of James.

In the eighteenth century Pietist Christianity found its way to the American colonies and was an important stimulus to the religious revival known as the Great Awakening. In a real sense Pietism has shaped most of American Protestantism, but its greatest influence has been felt among Protestants of the Wesleyan theological persuasion. This group includes the several Methodist bodies as well as the Wesleyan Church, the Church of the Nazarene, the Church of God (Anderson), and others. Historically these church groups have taught believers that discipleship entails a particular lifestyle. In the words of James, followers of Jesus must not only hear the word; it must also be practiced.

Option 1 (Little Prep)

Participate in an observation activity.

Distribute copies of "What Do You See?" (Reproducible 1) or show it as a projection. Next, pass out paper and pens or pencils. Allow students twenty seconds or so to carefully study the handout; then collect it and ask the following questions. Students should record the answers on their own:

Warm Up

- **What did the sign on the fence say?** NO CLIMBING (upside down)
- **What were the scores on the scoreboard?** 0 to 0
- **What letters were on the players' hats?** A and B
- **What animal is in the picture?** A horse
- **What musical instrument is in the picture?** A violin
- **What flag was flying on the flagpole?** The American flag (upside down)
- **What object was serving as home base?** It looks like a bowl or offering plate

After everyone has had a chance to respond to the questions, provide the correct answers. How did your students do? Was anyone able to remember all the details?

Say, **It's tough to remember details about something we are not familiar with.**

Option 2 (More Prep)

Play a memory game.

Prior to class, prepare a tray covered with many different types of common household items (e.g., a pencil, a DVD, an apple, a key, and so forth). Cover the tray with a towel so it is not visible to the students. Divide the class into three separate groups and ask the groups to move so that they are not close to one another. Let the first group look at the items on the tray for ten seconds; then recover the tray. Ask this group to quickly write down all the items they can remember and then submit their paper. Next, allow the second group *twenty* seconds to observe the tray; then ask them to quickly write down all the items they can remember and submit their list. Finally, allow the last group to observe the tray for *thirty* seconds, then ask them to quickly take note of what they saw and submit their list. Only allow about ten seconds for any group to recall and make their list. Compare the papers. Did the group with the longest time to observe remember more? Ask why this would be expected. Encourage the students to discuss their feelings about the activity. Were the first groups frustrated by being given less time? What were some techniques they used to try to remember what items were on the tray? Were they surprised by what they could remember or disappointed that they could not remember more?

Say, **It's tough to remember details about something we don't have much time to study.**

Note:

If you sent the Portable Sanctuary home with students last week, take some time at the beginning of this session to review and discuss their experience.

Starting Line

OPTION 1 (YOUNGER YOUTH)

Dramatize a parable.

Invite the students to turn to Matthew 21:28–32 and ask them to dramatize the parable told by Christ in a contemporary manner. Depending on class size and time, you could divide into groups to do this or select a few volunteers. Encourage students to creatively change the location and events but retain the message of the parable.

After the skits are presented, encourage your students to explain the main message of the parable. Ask, **What is more obedient and pleasing to God—words or actions?** This parable is very simple, but it makes the point clearly: God calls us to action, and action is what he expects.

When you are ready to move on, say, **Let's see what God's Word says about being active in our journey of faith.**

. . . .

OPTION 2 (OLDER YOUTH)

Discuss things we know but do not apply.

Write on one half of the board some general facts that are known but often not applied. Here are some examples:

- *Flossing adds seven years to your life.*
- *Eating a balanced diet is healthy for you.*
- *Wearing sunscreen protects your skin from cancer.*
- *Driving over the speed limit can be dangerous.*
- *Eating a good breakfast can increase alertness in school.*

Invite the students to add to the list. Now, on the other side of the board write reasons why these facts are not applied in everyday life. Is it laziness? lack of time? too expensive? something else? Ask the students to then determine which reasons are valid and which are not. Circle the reasons that are identified as valid and cross out the ones that are not.

When you are ready to move on, say, **Let's see what God's Word says about following God's instructions.**

Leading through the Session

Straight Away

Explore the Bible passage.

Distribute copies of "A Scripture Study: James 1:16–27" (Reproducible 2) and ask the students to pair up. In their pairs, the students should dissect the passage, using the handout to list the things that James said to do. Students should then identify specific ways they could put James's instructions into action in their own lives.

After several minutes, invite the students to share their responses as you take notes on the board. Here are suggested answers for "Things to Do":

- *Be quick to listen*

- *Be slow to anger*
- *Get rid of moral filth and evil*
- *Humbly accept the word*
- *Don't just listen to the word*
- *Do what the word says*
- *Continue to look intently into the perfect law*
- *Don't forget what you have heard*
- *Keep a tight reign on your tongue*
- *Take care of orphans and widows*
- *Keep yourself from being polluted by the world*

Go over your summary and ask, **From this passage, what can we determine to be the desire of God for his people?** We should help and care for those less fortunate, and really do what the Bible says instead of just talking about it. Remind the students that actions speak louder than words and thus are a greater testimony to what we believe.

Say, **James taught that words without actions are meaningless.**

The Turn

Discuss the need to obey God's Word.

Invite a student to read Romans 2:13. Ask, **Who will be considered righteous in God's sight?** Those who actually obey the law and not those who just hear the law. Invite another student to read Matthew 7:21. Ask, **What is the point Christ made in this verse?** It is not enough to claim to have a relationship with Christ. What will matter in the end is whether or not we lived for God and obeyed his Word. Ask students to compare these two verses. Invite another student to read Luke 6:46–49. Discuss the following questions:

- **What do you think the flood represents?** Possibly the many trials and difficulties that come into our lives.
- **How can following God's commandments help us stand against the flood?** By following the Word of God, we can find strength to persevere in such situations.
- **What happens to the foundation of a person who does not obey God's commandments?** The foundation is weak, so this person's faith crumbles apart; his or her life is shattered.

Now invite a student to read John 13:17. Ask, **What is the result of doing the things that Christ instructs?** We will be blessed. Invite students to discuss other possible results of obeying God's commandments. Some possibilities:

- Our lives will be a witness. Others will know that we are Christians by our love and how we model Christ.
- God will accomplish his purposes through us.
- We will grow personally in Christ.

Say, **When we act in obedience, others are blessed—and so are we.**

Home Stretch

OPTION 1 (YOUNGER YOUTH)

Confess personal hardships to one another.

Invite your students to partner with another student with whom they feel they can comfortably share. If the class does not know each other well, you can instead invite students to participate in private introspection. Say, **Consider your life in connection to what we have studied in James. Are there any areas where you are struggling in your pursuit to live as Christ? What do you struggle with the most? Why is it so difficult? What could you do to obey in these issues?** Ask the students to pray for one another. Point out that as we share these burdens, others can support us in the journey, through prayer, accountability, and in other practical ways.

When you are ready to move on, say, **God wants to help you better understand and follow his commands.**

· ·

OPTION 2 (OLDER YOUTH)

Determine areas of needed growth.

Invite the students to look again at "A Scripture Study: James 1:16–27" (Reproducible 2). Encourage them to spend a few quiet moments before God, asking the Holy Spirit to convict them of any area where they are neglecting to follow God. Perhaps the Holy Spirit will bring something to mind that is not even present in this text. Ask the students to confess to God their need to grow in these areas and to ask for God's help. After this time of reflection, provide an opportunity for them to share their revelations with a partner if possible. They should discuss plans for how they are going to work on these areas. Invite the students to pray for and encourage one another.

When you are ready to move on, say, **God wants to help you better understand and follow his commands.**

Finish Line

OPTION 1 (LITTLE PREP)

Discuss faithful responses.

Read the following scenarios to the students (they are also available on the Digital BRIDGES CD as a projection). After reading each scenario, encourage a time of discussion.

Scenario One:

Erika, a girl in your class, has gone through significant changes in the past month. She does not seem to care much about school, although she used to. She is usually sullen, and her appearance seems neglected. One day last week, she had a black eye. You asked her if she was okay, but she told you to butt out and leave her alone. When you saw her go through the cafeteria line earlier you noticed that she pulled out just a few coins from her pocket for a carton

of milk. You feel concerned for her. Even though Erika is unreceptive to help, how could you put your faith into action to reach out to her? How could you respond as Christ would without driving Erika farther away?

Scenario Two:

Jared is furious with you because you refused to give him the answers for last night's math homework. When you went to leave for home today you found that all the air had been let out of the tires of your car. Someone had also smeared mud all over the sides and back of the car. As you stand in disbelief, staring at your car, Jared whistles at you across the parking lot: "Oh…nice car!! Bee-u-tifullll! See what happens when you don't help your friends?" As he drives off you feel your blood boiling and your temperature rising. How would you naturally want to respond in this type of situation? How *could* you respond to Jared as a faithful follower of Christ? Is such a response possible or realistic?

After these discussions, ask the students if they have personal examples to share about times when they put faith into action. How did God honor that choice? Encourage them to think about how God would like them to act when they face challenging situations in life.

Close the session in prayer, asking for courage for the students so that they can put faith into action in a broken world.

. . . .

OPTION 2 (MORE PREP)

Plan and implement a ministry trip.

Remind the students of James 1:27. Religion that pleases God involves caring for and serving others, particularly those in the greatest need such as widows and orphans. Remind the students that when they serve others, they are serving Christ. Brainstorm to generate ideas for ways that your group could minister to the needy. (You might want to aid this process by researching opportunities in the area prior to class and making suggestions to the students.) Consider opportunities for service at places that might involve widows or orphans, such as food banks, orphanages, and homeless shelters. If possible, try to go to minister within the coming week, so the concept of "faith in action" can be reinforced in your students' minds and they can see it realized in their lives. (Even something as simple as babysitting for a single mom or spending time with a kid who has no dad around could be a blessing.)

Close the session in prayer, asking for courage for the students so that they can put faith into action in a broken world.

Note:

Don't forget to distribute copies of the Portable Sanctuary to students before they go.

What Do You See?

A Scripture Study: James 1:16—27

As you read the text, fill in the chart below.

Things to Do	How can you follow this in your life?

Portable Sanctuary

Day 1
Tough Living

There is a famous quote of Mohandas Gandhi that has gotten a lot of exposure recently in Christian literature. The gist of the quote is that if Christians really truly lived out the teachings of Christ, then the world would be a better place (and many other people would be drawn to following Christ). This brings to mind the question, Why aren't Christians *living* their faith? The reason is that it is much easier not to. The devil encourages us that just attending church or hearing the Word is enough. It is not—we've also got to live it.

Questions and Suggestions

• If someone had the ability to watch you but never heard you speak, could he or she tell by your lifestyle that you are a Christian? Do you actively demonstrate your faith in your daily life?

• Pray, asking God to help you live daily as a follower of Christ.

Day 2
Not Just Works

Good works are important—but the Christian life is not just about doing good things. Some people think, "God will love me more if I help others." Acts of service seem to be the way to guarantee God's approval, and in some cases people believe that it's the key to their salvation. This is a key belief in other faiths. For example, Muslims believe that in order to go to paradise your good deeds must outweigh your bad deeds—sort of like a "cosmic scorecard"! Hindus and Buddhists also contend that doing good deeds can bring you to a higher level when you are reincarnated.

Imagine the uncertainty of your eternal future as you try to measure up. We cannot be saved by our works.

Questions and Suggestions

- Read Ephesians 2:8–9. How are we saved? Why are we not saved by our works?
- Pray that God will give you the assurance in your faith to do many good works in love.

Day 3
Perfect Harmony

There can be harmony between faith and works. Our faith in God is the basis of our salvation. However, because we have been saved, we are able to share this love with others. The joy of our salvation through Christ is like a fountain that wells up within us. Because we have faith in God and love him, we are compelled to do that which is pleasing to God. We do not do good works because we *have* to, but because we *want* to. It comes out of our love for God, who has saved us.

Questions and Suggestions

- Read Ephesians 2:10. God has things planned for you to do. Will you join him at work in the world? How do you see yourself ministering out of love for God?
- Write down your thoughts regarding the relationship between faith and good works.

Day 4
Doers, Not Just Hearers

Imagine if all the teens who are taking driver's education this year just said, "Oh, that was great information! I'm so glad they told us about it, but I really don't need to follow those rules to the letter. Some of it seems a little too hard to keep track of. I'll just do what I want. If it suits me I'll do it, but what I do or don't do doesn't really matter."

Imagine the chaos that would ensue and the lives that could be lost! It is sobering to realize that if we just listen to God's Word but do not do what it says, lives could be lost too—for eternity!

Questions and Suggestions

- Read James 2:14–26. Is it possible to just have faith in God and not have good deeds come from that? Consider your life for a moment. Are you doing what the Lord has asked of you?
- Write down some deeds that you need to be doing. Commit to the Lord that you will follow his directions.

Day 5
The Word

The Word of God gives life. It is "living and active. Sharper than any double-edged sword, it penetrates even to dividing soul and spirit, joints and marrow; it judges the thoughts and attitudes of the heart" (Hebrew 4:12). Not only does the Word of God give us a glimpse of who God is through his interactions with God's people, but it convicts our hearts and minds and directs us to live a life pleasing to the Lord. The Word of God is essential for our life journey. It goes right to the heart.

Questions and Suggestions

- Take a look at how often James mentions *the Word* in James 1:16–27. Make a note of the importance of the Word according to James. How has God's Word impacted your life?
- If you have access to a concordance, seek other verses that describe the Word of God. What do you learn?

Leading into the Session

Warm Up

Option 1 Identify favorite things.
LITTLE PREP *Reproducible 1, pens or pencils*
Option 2 Participate in a tasting activity.
MORE PREP *"Altered" snack foods*

Starting Line

Option 1 Participate in an activity of exclusion.
YOUNGER YOUTH
Option 2 Discuss *favoritism.*
OLDER YOUTH *Chalkboard or dry erase board*

Leading through the Session

Straight Away

Explore the Bible passage.
Bibles

The Turn

Dramatize the story of the good Samaritan.
Bibles

Leading beyond the Session

Home Stretch

Option 1 Discuss covenant relationships with God.
YOUNGER YOUTH *Rings that can be written on, fine-point markers*
Option 2 Analyze covenant relationships with God.
OLDER YOUTH *Reproducible 2, pens or pencils*

Finish Line

Option 1 Identify ways to live a life pleasing to God.
LITTLE PREP *Chalkboard or dry erase board*
Option 2 Determine ways to restore a right relationship with God.
MORE PREP *Band-Aids, fine-point markers*

SESSION 2

NO FAVORITES

Bible Passage
James 2:1–13

Key Verse
Have you not made distinctions among yourselves, and become judges with evil thoughts?
—James 2:4, NRSV

Main Thought
All people should be treated equally, as loved creations of God.

133

Bible Background

When the prophet Samuel chose from Jesse's sons the one who would be king in Israel, the first to appear before him was Eliab. Tall and handsome, his impressive physical features immediately convinced Samuel that this was the man God had chosen. But God rejected Eliab, explaining to Samuel, "The LORD does not see as man sees; men judge by appearances, but the LORD judges by the heart" (1 Sam 16:7, NEB). Samuel shared the tendency to judgment by superficial criteria with all human beings. We are warned not to judge books by their covers, and the letter of James teaches a similar lesson when it comes to the people of God.

Most of what we know of the socio-economic status of early Christians is based on very sketchy data. Some wealthy people followed Jesus; Joseph of Arimathea could afford a tomb carved from rock, far more elegant than the burial places of most of Jesus' followers. Nevertheless, Joseph appears to have been the exception rather than the rule. Jesus' earliest followers were "people of the land," men and women at the bottom of the social scale. As the gospel spread beyond Judea and Samaria into the uttermost parts of the world it encountered a Roman culture where poor people and slaves comprised the vast majority of the population. Only after Constantine and his mother Helena converted did Christianity acquire wealthy patrons at the top of society who spent lavishly on building churches, duplicating manuscript Bibles, and funding church budgets. Late in the first century, it seems that the percentage of wealthy Christians did not exceed the percentage of wealthy people in the general population; there is reason to estimate that percentage to have been lower. These thoughts help us understand James's caution for Christians on the somewhat rare occasion when a man or woman entered the assembly wearing obvious signs of wealth. As with the Lord's advice to Samuel, James urged his readers not to be fooled by outward appearances.

Our ears open prematurely in the presence of wealth or, correlatively, fame. They instantly build a platform from which their bearers speak, whether or not they have something to say. It is worth remembering that neither wealth nor fame disqualify a person from our respect, but neither are they the basis for it. Thus the fourth-century Christian Hilary of Arles condemned any form of discrimination: "It is a sin to show any class distinction among persons, for the law says: 'You shall not be partial in judgment, you shall bear the small and the great alike.' Jesus confirmed this when he said: 'Do not judge by appearances, but judge with right judgment.'"[1] Neither wealth nor poverty is an automatic proof of wisdom or holiness. Not every poor person is a Francis of Assisi. And we would be just as mistaken to automatically favor the wealthy or famous over men and women who are poor, but learned and wise in the ways of God.

1. Gerald Bray, ed., *James; 1—2 Peter, 1—3 John, Jude,* from the series Ancient Christian Commentary on Scripture: New Testament, Vol. XI (Downers Grove: InterVarsity Press, 2000), 24.

Option 1 (Less Prep)

Identify favorite things.

Distribute copies of "My Favorite Things" (Reproducible 1) and invite the students to complete the questionnaire. After a few minutes, invite the class members to share some of their favorite things with the rest of the group. As they share, you may wish to ask some students *why* they chose those particular things. Ask the whole group, **What helps you make a decision as to which things are your favorites? How do you decide?** If you know the song "My Favorite Things" from *The Sound of Music*, feel free to do a solo for your class.

Say, **We all have "favorites"—things we enjoy more than other things.**

Warm Up

- -

Option 2 (More Prep)

Participate in a tasting activity.

Prepare a few types of snack food for class. Think about how you can alter these snacks so that they look terrible but still taste good. For example, you can use food coloring to turn chip dip bright green, ketchup black, and marshmallows dirty brown. Invite the students to sample the snacks you have prepared. If anyone hesitates, ask why they are uncertain about trying the food. Assure them that it still tastes good, regardless of how it looks. After some students have been willing to try the snacks, encourage them to share a description of how it tastes. Point out that appearances can be deceiving. Ask, **Have you ever seen something that you thought for sure was bad, but it turned out to be good—or vice versa?** Invite the students to share their experiences.

Say, **We all have "favorites"—things we enjoy more than other things.**

> *Note:*
>
> If you sent the Portable Sanctuary home with students last week, take some time at the beginning of this session to review and discuss their experience.

Option 1 (Younger Youth)

Participate in an activity of exclusion.

Prior to class, think of a good-tempered student to be the subject of this activity. As you begin a discussion about favoritism, make every effort to be rude to that one student. You can ignore, interrupt, and generally harass this person. Include the other students in the discussion, but pointedly treat the one student poorly. After allowing some time for the students to feel the effect of this treatment, open the topic for discussion. Ask the excluded person, **How did you feel about the way I treated you? Did it surprise you?** Ask the other students, **What did you think about the way I treated this person? Why did you or why did you not say anything about it?** Point out that most of us would want someone to say something on our behalf if we were being treated poorly.

When you are ready to move on, say, **Let's see what the Bible says about how we interact with and treat one another.**

Starting Line

Option 2 (Older Youth)

Discuss favoritism.

Write the word *favoritism* in the center of the board. Invite the students to take turns writing on the board what they feel when they read that word. Ask, **What does the word *favoritism* bring to mind?** After you have generated some good thoughts, analyze them together by discussing the following questions:

- **Are our impressions of favoritism mostly negative?**
- **Do you think favoritism is biblical? Why or why not?**
- **Are you familiar with any biblical passages that demonstrate favoritism?** One example: Genesis 37:3 states clearly that Jacob favored Joseph over his other sons.
- **When have *you* experienced favoritism (from either side)? What was it like?**

When you are ready to move on, say, **Let's see what the Bible says about favoritism and how we should interact with one another.**

Leading through the Session

Straight Away

Explore the Bible passage.

Read together James 2:1–13 and discuss the following questions:

- **Whom was James writing to?** To his "brothers"—fellow believers in Jesus. Point out that these instructions include things that should be expected of *Christians*.
- **What example of favoritism did James use? How is this such an "evil" thing?** James mentioned showing special attention to a rich person who comes to church, to the extent of giving this person a good seat but making a poor person sit on the floor. When we discriminate in this way we are "judging" one person to be better than another based on appearances. It is unwise to be blinded by material things and disregard the equality of all people in God's sight.
- **What did James say about who is *really* rich?** Those who are poor by the world's standards are rich in faith, chosen to inherit God's kingdom. Point out that the poor can be more dependent on God. They have a greater tendency to put their trust in God and his provision, since they don't have money and material possessions to depend on.
- **What do the "worldly" rich people do that is so bad?** They exploit (take advantage of) others and slander Christ. Sometimes the rich feel that they do not need God because they are able to provide for themselves. They are more interested in their own wealth and position than in God, and they use others to achieve their success.
- **Where have you heard the "royal law" before?** "Love your neighbor as yourself" (Leviticus 19:18) was quoted by Jesus in Matthew 22:39 as the second-greatest commandment in all the Law. These words are quoted frequently, even outside of church circles, as a good way to live.

- **If we show favoritism, what are we guilty of?** We are sinning and breaking God's law—and even breaking one single point of the law makes us guilty.
- **Do you believe that one type of sin is worse than another? How do you feel about the fact that someone who commits favoritism is as guilty before God as someone who commits murder?** In our minds we like to have a hierarchy—we like to put a grade or value on things. We like to rank sins and fool ourselves that we are better than others because we do not commit terrible sins. However, to God, all sins are the same.
- **As believers, how should we speak and act?** As those who are being judged under the law of freedom. In a way, our actions determine how we ourselves will be judged by God. If we have shown mercy to others, we can expect to receive God's mercy.

Say, **All people are equal in God's sight and should be treated equally.**

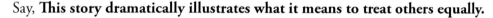

Dramatize the story of the good Samaritan.

Mention again the "royal law" found in James 2:8: "Love your neighbor as yourself." Invite the students to read Luke 10:29. Say, **Someone once asked Jesus to identify just who qualifies as a neighbor.** Jesus responded with a story, a parable that is familiar to many people. Remind your students of the story: two pious religious people would not help a man in need. However, a Samaritan, an enemy of the Jews, showed mercy to the injured man. Ask your students to identify the main point of the story: *All* people are our neighbors. We should not show preference or favoritism to anyone; God has called us to show mercy and love to all. Divide the class into small groups to enact a modern good Samaritan story. Ask, **In today's society who would be expected to show mercy? Who would be perceived as unlikely to reach out?** Invite the groups to share their skits with the class. (Luke 10:25–37 can be referenced if necessary.)

Say, **This story dramatically illustrates what it means to treat others equally.**

The Turn

Leading beyond the Session

OPTION 1 (YOUNGER YOUTH)

Discuss covenant relationships with God.

Review the concept of covenant with your students. In our relationship with God, we have made promises to God and God to us. Under this covenant, God has saved us and we in turn submit ourselves to him. It's a two-way relationship. When we don't do the things God has asked of us, or when we sin, our relationships with him are broken. Bring to class some inexpensive rings that can be written on (something from a craft store will do; you could even cut some "rings" out of construction paper). Hold up a ring and ask, **When are rings most often exchanged?** At weddings, symbolizing the covenant promises made between the bride and groom. The perfect and unending circle of a ring is symbolic of a covenant working the way it should—unbroken. However, when we sin and

Home Stretch

disappoint God, our relationships with him are disrupted—like denting or tearing the ring. Even a small sin such as favoritism distances us from God.

Distribute rings to the students. Invite the class to spend some time in quiet reflection before God, asking him to reveal to them the status of their relationships with him. If there is something that has caused a break in the relationship, students can use fine-point markers to write a short description of the sin on their rings.

When you are ready to move on, say, **Put this ring someplace where that it will remind you to mend your covenant with God. When you have mended the covenant, mark out the writing on the ring or throw the ring away.**

· ·

OPTION 2 (OLDER YOUTH)

Analyze covenant relationships with God.

Invite the students to a time of silent reflection. Distribute copies of "Real-Life Questions" (Reproducible 2) and ask the students to use part of their reflection time to ponder and answer the questions on the handout. After a few minutes, ask willing students to share some of their responses. Do not pressure anyone to share, but provide a trusting and prayerful environment where students can feel open and not threatened.

When you are ready to move on, say, **If we have shown favoritism or done anything else to damage our relationships with God, God is waiting to heal and restore.**

Finish Line

Note:

Don't forget to distribute copies of the Portable Sanctuary to students before they go.

OPTION 1 (LITTLE PREP)

Identify ways to live a life pleasing to God.

Perhaps today God has brought to your students' minds some behaviors or attitudes that are not pleasing to God. Perhaps God brought to mind favoritism or something else. Point out that *any* sin distances us from God and his plans for our lives. Say, **Now that you have identified some issues, where do you go from here? What kind of choices can you make that bring glory to God?** Draw the outline of a large pair of feet, complete with toes, on the chalkboard or dry erase board. Read Micah 6:8 aloud: **He has showed you, O man [and woman!], what is good. And what does the LORD require of you? To act justly and to love mercy and to walk humbly with your God.** Invite the students to fill in the feet you have drawn with practical ideas of how to move ahead in their areas of difficulty. What is God calling them to do? Challenge the students to choose two or three of these ideas to implement during the week.

Close the session by praying that God will help your students walk in his ways.

OPTION 2 (MORE PREP)

Determine ways to restore a right relationship with God.

Pass out Band-Aids and fine-point markers to the students. The Band-Aids may be small, but should be big enough for students to write on. Say, **Think about something that has broken or damaged your relationship with God.** Ask the students to think about one or two practical steps they could take to restore their relationships with God and walk away from the sin that has caused the separation. They should write these steps on the Band-Aids and then place them on their fingers as a reminder.

Close by inviting your students to pray in pairs that their relationships with God will be restored. They should also pray specifically about not showing favoritism and about loving their neighbors.

Note:

Don't forget to distribute copies of the Portable Sanctuary to students before they go.

SPREAD THE STW WORD

TEENAGERS SPREADING THE GOSPEL AROUND THE WORLD

www.chogy.org

Key verse:

"And how can they preach unless they are sent? As it is written, 'How beautiful are the feet of those who bring good news!'" Romans 10:15 (NIV)

Goal:

A North American missions avenue to enable youth to spread the Kingdom around the globe through financial giving.

Focus:

Spread the Word gives specifically to tools for evangelism. This includes photocopiers, vehicles, bicycles, boats, trailers, tractors, planes, sound systems, audio and videocassette duplicators, tape-editing equipment, projectors, microphones, mules, oxen and carts, camels, and printed evangelistic materials. This could also include special projects with a youth emphasis, such as youth centers, or other ministries that are having an enormous effect on world evangelism.

General Requests

The following is a list of some items that are requested on a regular basis. (The amounts vary by region and request. The purpose here is to give a general idea of where funds are needed.)

Bike	$300	Canoe	$500
Generator	$1,000	Computer	$1,500
Literature	$1,500	Motorcycle	$2,000
Video Projector	$3,000	Minivan	$15,000

For More Info:

Visit: www.chogy.org (click on the STW logo)
E-mail: STW@chog.org
Call: 800-848-2464, ext. 2156

To Give:

Online: www.chogy.org (click on the STW logo)
By Mail: Spread the Word
         Church of God Ministries
         PO Box 2420
         Anderson, IN 46018

My Favorite Things

Identify your favorite things in the blanks below and then be ready to share your responses with the class.

1. My favorite color is _____ .

2. My favorite food is _____ .

3. My favorite actor or actress is _____ .

4. My favorite movie is _____ .

5. My favorite song is _____ .

6. My favorite type of music is _____ .

7. My favorite day of the week is _____ .

7. My favorite sport is _____ .

8. My favorite season is _____ .

9. My favorite holiday is _____ .

10. My favorite weekend activity is _____ .

11. My favorite meal of the day is _____ .

12. My favorite subject in school is _____ .

13. My favorite animal is _____ .

14. My favorite teacher is _____ .

15. My favorite TV show is _____ .

16. My favorite candy is _____ .

17. My favorite dessert is _____ .

18. My favorite cartoon is _____ .

19. My favorite soda pop is _____ .

20. My favorite musical instrument is _____ .

Real-Life Questions

Search me, O God, and know my heart; test me and know my anxious thoughts. See if there is any offensive way in me, and lead me in the way everlasting. —Psalm 139:23–24

Pray the verses above before answering the questions below, asking God to speak to you as you examine your heart and mind.

1. Have you ever shown favoritism? If so, describe a time you showed favoritism.

_____

_____

_____

2. How was that damaging to the person you did not favor, to yourself, or to others?

_____

_____

_____

3. Right now, how would you rate your relationship with God? (Circle a response)

Growing and strong   Broken   I am not sure

Neglected   Something else: _____

4. Have you done things recently that have broken God's heart? Ask God to bring to mind anything that has disappointed him. What impact has that choice made on your relationship with God?

_____

_____

_____

5. Write the prayer of your heart below. Perhaps you need to pray a prayer of confession, a prayer asking for help, or a prayer of thanksgiving. Share your heart with God.

_____

_____

_____

Portable Sanctuary

Day 1

The Lure of Money

One of Satan's most effective tools in the lives of people is materialism. People work and strive to get more. The wealth carrot dangled in front of their noses screams, "Come get it! If you can get enough, then surely you will be happy!" But there is never enough, for wealth cannot satisfy. Wealth attracts us and traps us. Favoritism is shown to the wealthy because it is hoped that the wealth and influence will be shared. But often times the wealth is not shared, for the wealthy cannot even get enough (Ecclesiastes 5:10). Beware of money and great wealth, for it can quickly block your growth in your journey of faith (Matthew 6:24).

Questions and Suggestions

• Is there any way for the wealthy to truly have communion with God? How do you think this can be accomplished?

• If you have access to a concordance, look up different occurrences of *riches*, *wealth*, and *money* in the Bible. Take notes on what the Bible says about them.

Day 2

The Effects of Sin

It is really difficult to put some moments of sinfulness behind us. When we hurt someone deeply, sometimes those relationships never recover. Because the relationships are so damaged, you may feel lingering guilt—even though the moment is passed. Showing favoritism can do that type of damage. When you put someone over another person, you are essentially saying to the other person, "You do not matter—you are not

Questions and Suggestions

• How can prejudice and discrimination be addressed within the church and the world? How can you personally make a difference?

• Look up a news article regarding a situation of prejudice or discrimination in the world. Take this situation to God, asking for his intervention.

N O T E S

"important!" As a result, that person leaves a relationship with you with a heart aching and bleeding. Although you may confess to this person and God and beg forgiveness, the relationship may be lost forever. Treat one another carefully, with love and respect, so that the body of Christ may grow and not be torn apart.

Questions and Suggestions
• How does it feel to be hurt by another person? How does it feel to cause others pain?
• Pray that God will give you the ability to love everyone equally.

Day 3
Fruit of the Spirit
When a healthy plant is growing it produces fruit. Fruit is a product of its life. If a plant is not growing properly, it will not bear fruit. Likewise, if a plant is growing properly it can be very fruitful. The fruit that is produced is contingent upon the type of plant. An orange tree cannot bear coconuts! Christians too bear fruit. If we are in a growing relationship with Christ, then much fruit will be produced (John 15:5–6). What is this fruit that is produced when we are growing in Christ? Love, joy, peace, patience, kindness, goodness, faithfulness, gentleness, and self-control (Galatians 5:22–23).

Questions and Suggestions
• Have you seen good fruit produced in your life since you began your walk with Christ? What needs to be developed further?
• Ask God to help the fruit of the Spirit develop in you.

Day 4
A Treasured Possession
She giggled as she softly whispered into the doll's ear, its waxy hair rumpled under a soft pink bonnet. All the secrets of her tiny heart came pouring into that listening plastic ear. Although the dress was ragged and the arm pulling out of the socket, the doll was still deeply loved. If it was not lying on her pillow, sitting in her wagon, or present at her tea party, the world would dissolve into a sea of tears. It was treasured, a part of her heart. We are God's treasured possessions. God said in Exodus 19:5 that if we will fully obey him and *keep his covenant*, then out of all the people of the world we will be his "treasured possession." God treasures us so much that he even sent his only Son to die for us and redeem us from our sins (John 3:16).

Questions and Suggestions
• What is your most treasured possession? Can you believe that you matter so much to God that he would be willing to die for you (John 15:12–13)?
• Thank God for sending his Son to die for you. Thank God for treasuring you. Commit to walking in covenant with God.

Day 5
A World of Hate
Our world is filled with prejudice, discrimination, and hatred. If you crack open a history book you can see the impact of this on innocent lives—the African slave trade, the Jews of the Nazi period, the Bosnian-Serbian conflict, the Rwandan turmoil. The initial flames of discrimination or prejudice have often blown into violent conflicts where millions have died. In a world like this, where is love? How can Christians stand apart—being different and showing love where there is no love?

Leading into the Session

Warm Up

Option 1
LITTLE PREP
Create and say tongue twisters.
Reproducible 1; candy or other small prizes (optional)

Option 2
MORE PREP
Participate in tongue competitions.
Starburst-type candies, cherries, small straws

Starting Line

Option 1
YOUNGER YOUTH
Observe training and taming.
A dog trainer or animal trainer with a subject in training; Digital BRIDGES CD, computer, and data projector (optional)

Option 2
OLDER YOUTH
Discuss the power of words.
Chalkboard or dry erase board

Leading through the Session

Straight Away

Explore the Bible passage.
Bibles, chalkboard or dry erase board

The Turn

Discuss wise speech.
Bibles

Leading beyond the Session

Home Stretch

Option 1
YOUNGER YOUTH
Express thanks for wisdom and guidance.
Thank-you cards, pens or pencils, chalkboard or dry erase board

Option 2
OLDER YOUTH
Share about the power of speech.
Chalkboard or dry erase board

Finish Line

Option 1
LITTLE PREP
Discuss "What I Want" with a partner.
Reproducible 2, pens or pencils

Option 2
MORE PREP
Create a reminder to live according to the Word.
Various colors of thread and beads, scissors

SESSION 3

TAMING THE TONGUE

Bible Passage
James 3

Key Verse
Who is wise and understanding among you? Show by your good life that your works are done with gentleness born of wisdom.
—James 3:13, NRSV

Main Thought
Heavenly wisdom should influence our lives and our speech.

Bible Background

King Henry II of England is not as well-remembered today as is his more famous son, Richard I "the Lionhearted." Henry did not take the crusader's cross, but he was the more able of the two rulers and brought stability to eleventh- and early twelfth-century England. Henry is also remembered for a rhetorical question he asked within earshot of some of his henchmen. The question, "Will no one rid me of this meddlesome priest?" may have been calculated on Henry's part. Whether calculated or an offhand remark, the question nonetheless carried deadly effect. It led directly to the murder of Henry's friend and former confidant Archbishop Thomas Becket while he stood near the altar of Canterbury Cathedral.

The power to build or destroy is not restricted to the tongues of kings. Indeed it is well nigh universal. Many of us can remember a moment when we wished we could pull our own hurtful words out of the air before they reached anyone's ears, and we can just as well recall brightening a person's day with a word of blessing. How illustrative of all the potential of human existence is the tongue! Human beings have developed healing medicines and vaccines that have made life safer for the whole planet. They have created artistic works of indescribable beauty. The same human race has raped, pillaged, and murdered its way across the pages of history. Perhaps we should not be surprised at the tongue's power to wound or heal; it is the organ in which all a man or woman's potential for good or evil exists in perhaps the most concentrated form.

James holds out a particular warning for teachers. Their calling means that the effects of their speech will be multiplied perhaps manyfold. James's metaphor of the ship's rudder is especially apt in their case. One teacher instructs a class of thirty, who each in turn repeat this instruction to another thirty. Only one "student generation" from the teacher some nine hundred people have now been influenced by his or her instruction. Teaching carries an awesome responsibility. Most of us are prepared to live by our convictions, but teaching opens the possibility that our students may also choose to live by them. To teach means that we may watch others reap the benefits or suffer the consequences of what we have taught.

James 3 is finally a call to Christian integrity. We are to be, so to speak, cut from whole cloth. Rather than a patchwork of some good and some wickedness, some laudable attitudes and others that are not, James calls us to a life of good deeds consistent with heavenly wisdom. Such wisdom is not arcane or mysterious; it is not difficult to find. If anyone should wonder, James listed its characteristics—peace-loving, submissive, full of mercy, and so forth. This wisdom stands in marked contrast to the wisdom of the world. One thinks immediately of Bunyan's "Mr. Worldly Wiseman" in *The Pilgrim's Progress*, whose bad advice steers Christian off the path that leads to the Celestial City. Worldly wisdom and heavenly wisdom mix no better than oil and water. James appeals to us to choose the true wisdom, live wholly Christian lives, and stay on the right path.

Option 1 (Little Prep)

Create and say tongue twisters.

Distribute copies of "Tongue-Tied" (Reproducible 1) or show it as a projection and invite the students to practice saying the common tongue twisters on the handout. Next, invite the students to pair up. Challenge these pairs to create their own original tongue twisters and share them with the rest of the class. If you wish, you can award candy or other small prizes to the pair who creates the most popular or difficult tongue twister.

Say, **Some of you have impressive tongue capabilities!**

Warm Up

Option 2 (More Prep)

Participate in tongue competitions.

Conduct some "tongue competitions" with your students. Here are some suggestions:

- See who can roll their tongues.
- See who can flip their tongues over upside down.
- See who can touch their noses with their tongues.
- See who can unwrap a Starburst-type candy in his or her mouth (only using the tongue—no hands!)
- See who can tie a cherry stem in a knot with their tongues.
- See who can flip over small straws with their tongues.

Award some of the candies you have brought as a prize to the student who "wins" your competition.

Say, **Some of you have impressive tongue capabilities!**

Note:

If you sent the Portable Sanctuary home with students last week, take some time at the beginning of this session to review and discuss their experience.

Option 1 (Younger Youth)

Observe training and taming.

Arrange to have a dog trainer or some other type of animal trainer visit your class with one of his or her animal subjects. Ask this person to give a short demonstration or presentation about how animals are trained. Invite the students to ask questions of your guest regarding the process of animal training. Be sure your guest shares about the difficulties of training an animal and about the harm that can result if an animal is improperly trained or not trained at all.

When you are ready to move on, say, **Let's see what the Bible says about something that is difficult—if not impossible—to tame.**

Starting Line

Note: If you have access to the Digital BRIDGES CD, a computer, and a data projector, you can also show the video clip "Dog Training."

OPTION 2 (OLDER YOUTH)

Discuss the power of words.

On the board, write the phrase *Sticks and stones may break my bones, but words will never hurt me.* Ask, **Do you agree with this statement? Why or why not? How do you know if what you say is hurtful or offensive to someone else?** Some teens argue that profanity and obscene language are acceptable at their most basic level because they are just words. What do your students think about this position? What words are "off-limits"? Explain that words are powerful, especially when they have meaning to the one hearing them. Logically, a curse word in a foreign language will not offend a person who is ignorant of its meaning. However, when the meaning is understood it ceases to be just a word—it has the power to anger or hurt someone.

If time permits, have an honest discussion about swear words or other words students may haphazardly use without the knowledge of their meanings. You may want to enlist the assistance of the youth pastor or a mature older student to help discuss words that are popular at this time. Your class members may hear a lot of profanity at school or even at home. They may understand the meanings but may use these words naturally because they hear them so often. Invite the students to discuss why it is unhealthy to use such language.

When you are ready to move on, say, **Let's see what the Bible says about the power of the tongue and speech, and how using words requires wisdom.**

Leading through the Session

Straight Away

Explore the Bible passage.

Read together James 3:1–18. As the passage is read, invite a student to draw on the board cartoons representing the different metaphors used. Discuss the following questions:

- **Why should most people be cautious about teaching others?** Because teachers will be judged more strictly. Press the students to explain what this means, and why it is so. A teacher influences whole classrooms of students, who then go out and spread the things they have learned to others. In the context of this passage, the reference is to those who teach the Word of God; they carry great responsibility because their words impact the spiritual future of their students, and they will be judged *by God*.
- **According to this passage, which part of the body holds the greatest influence—and why?** The tongue, meaning the things we say. If a person can control his or her speech, then the rest of the body tends to remain pure.
- **How is the tongue like the bit on a horse or the rudder of a boat?** It is a very small part of the body that has a great impact on the rest of the body. Make sure your students understand what bits and rudders are and how they work. Invite the class to suggest other metaphors that could describe this point about the tongue.
- **How is the tongue like a fire?** It can lead the whole body to damnation and destruction; just a tiny word can quickly start a big problem. James even said that our words can be linked to hell itself!

- **How did James contrast the tongue to the animal kingdom?** Even the wildest animals can be captured and tamed (to an extent) by human beings, but the tongue is untamable—restless and full of deadly poison. Point out that poorly chosen words can wound or kill a relationship, just as poison kills the body.
- **How did James contrast the tongue to water springs and plants?** A spring has either good water or bad water and a plant produces one kind of fruit, but the tongue is dualistic and hypocritical—praise and cursing come from the same mouth! Ask your students what their assessment is of a person who does both—praises God and curses others. Suggest that such behavior demonstrates a life not completely submitted to God, because God can control *all* parts of our lives—even our speech.
- **What is the difference between earthly wisdom and heavenly wisdom?** Earthly wisdom is envious and selfishly looks out for itself. Heavenly wisdom is pure, peace-loving, considerate, submissive, full of mercy and good fruit, impartial, and sincere. It is demonstrated in a person with a good life who does humble deeds.
- **What is the result when a person lives a peaceful life?** He or she reaps a harvest of righteousness—in other words, this person does what is right in God's eyes and helps others do the same.

Say, **When God is in control it makes a difference in our lives and our speech.**

Discuss wise speech.

Help your students to consider the relationship between wisdom and speech. Invite a volunteer to read Ecclesiastes 10:12. Ask, **How do the wise speak—and what happens to those who are not wise?** The wise speak with grace; those who are not wise are "consumed" by their speech. Remind students of the analogy of fire in James 3:6. Fire is consuming, and the wickedness of the tongue can destroy the speaker who is not wise in his or her speech. When we are guided by the wisdom that comes from above, it helps us live lives that are pleasing to God. One aspect of our lives that needs to be guided by that wisdom is the tongue.

The Turn

Divide the students into four groups and assign each group one of the following scriptures:

- Hebrews 13:15–16
- Colossians 3:17
- Colossians 4:6
- Ephesians 4:29—5:2

Ask the groups to discuss the meaning of the assigned passage. **How could this passage be applied to the life of a teen? How can we do what it says?** After providing time for reading and discussion, ask the groups to report their findings to the whole class.

Say, **Every time you study the Word of God, you have the chance to gain more of the godly wisdom you need.**

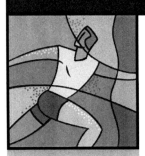

Home Stretch

OPTION 1 (YOUNGER YOUTH)

Express thanks for wisdom and guidance.

Remind your class of the characteristics of heavenly wisdom you have discussed today. Invite the students to think of a person who provides wisdom and guidance to them. Ask, **What are the characteristics of that person? How would you describe him or her?** As your students respond, write their ideas on the board. Distribute thank-you cards and encourage the students to write notes of thanks to these persons who provide them with wise guidance.

When you are ready to move on, say, **Be sure to mail or deliver your notes of thanks—and to thank God for those who share his wisdom with you.**

. . . .

OPTION 2 (OLDER YOUTH)

Share about the power of speech.

Invite the students to think about the power that words have had in their lives. Write the word *positive* on one side of the board and *negative* on the other side. Ask, **What was a time when someone said something kind or encouraging to you that really stuck with you? What was a time when someone said something hurtful that was not easily forgotten?** Invite the students to share these situations with one another. Perhaps not everyone will want to share about a painful experience, but encourage everyone to care for one another as they share. Point out that one person's story could help someone else become more sensitive to words that hurt and offend. If the Spirit moves, lead a time of prayer, asking God to heal hurts and help your students become encouraging and uplifting in their speech.

When you are ready to move on, say, **We all need God's help to think before we speak.**

Finish Line

OPTION 1 (LITTLE PREP)

Discuss "What I Want" with a partner.

Have the class members pair up. Distribute copies of "What I Want" (Reproducible 2) and ask the students to discuss the questions in their pairs. Point out that when God's children feel conviction in their hearts about things that need to change, that's the Holy Spirit speaking; Satan, the enemy, is pleased if we just leave things as they are. After their discussion, the students should pray for one another in their pairs.

Close the session by asking God to honor your students in their commitments to speak with godly wisdom and kindness.

> *Note:*
>
> Don't forget to distribute copies of the Portable Sanctuary to students before they go.

OPTION 2 (MORE PREP)

Create a reminder to live according to the Word.

Supply various colors of thread and invite the students to cut or take several strands of different colors. Explain that they will be making a bracelet or string to hang on their cell phones or key rings. As the students begin braiding their threads together, give each of them six colored beads. Explain that they will take turns threading a bead onto the string. The first person to put on a bead will say how he or she will be peace-loving. The rest should then take a turn expressing how they will be peace-loving as they thread the first bead. The first person then responds again, threading another bead and explaining how he or she will be considerate. The others should then take turns threading the next bead and explaining how they will be considerate. Do the same for *submissive, full of mercy, impartial,* and *careful with their speech.* After all six beads are threaded, the students should tie off and finish their creations. Challenge them to do what they have said during the coming week, using the physical reminders they have just made to help them strive after heavenly wisdom and live according to the Word of God. Say, **A good way to focus on godly speech is to say twenty positive things for every negative thing you find yourself saying.**

Close the session by asking God to honor your students in their commitments to speak with godly wisdom and kindness.

Note:

Don't forget to distribute copies of the Portable Sanctuary to students before they go.

Tongue-Tied

1. Peter Piper picked a peck of pickled peppers.
   Did Peter Piper pick a peck of pickled peppers?
   If Peter Piper picked a peck of pickled peppers,
   where's the peck of pickled peppers Peter Piper picked?

2. The sixth sick sheik's sixth sheep's sick.

3. Unique New York.

4. Black bug's blood.

5. Ned Nott was shot and Sam Shott was not.
   So it is better to be Shott than Nott.
   Some say Nott was not shot.
   But Shott says he shot Nott.
   Either the shot Shott shot at Nott was not shot, or Nott was shot.
   If the shot Shott shot shot Nott, Nott was shot.
   But if the shot Shott shot shot Shott, then Shott was shot, not Nott.
   However, the shot Shott shot shot not Shott—but Nott.

6. _____
   _____

7. _____
   _____

What I Want

Answer the following questions honestly and discuss your responses with your partner. Then pray for one another.

1. What word really discourages you? Why?

2. What words really encourage you? Why?

3. How do you wish to be treated in regard to the way others speak to you?

4. What do you struggle with in regard to your speech? What is God saying to you about this?

5. How do you feel about James's words on wisdom? What kind of wisdom do *you* need? Why?

6. James's list of characteristics resulting from heavenly wisdom includes *peace-loving, submissive, merciful, impartial,* and *sincere.* Which of these do you feel are your strengths? Which do you feel you need to concentrate on improving? How could you do that?

Portable Sanctuary

Day 1

The Source of All Wisdom

If someone were to ask you who the wisest person in the world is today, whom would you say? Does wisdom mean smart or intelligent? Those who try to become "wise" in the world today often throw themselves into written words, studying the combined knowledge of great minds. They also try to learn from other learned men and women in order to gain more insight. They are often older and have had many experiences in their lifetimes from which they have learned much. However, the Bible says that true wisdom comes from the Holy Spirit (1 John 2:20) and from the Word of God (2 Timothy 3:15). Solomon, the man who is credited with being the wisest man in all of history, received the gift of wisdom from the Lord (1 Kings 3:9). True wisdom is found in God.

Questions and Suggestions

• Spend some time reading the wisdom found in the Book of Proverbs. How can these verses be applied to your life? How useful is the wisdom found in the pages of that book?
• Pray that God will give you the gift of wisdom.

Day 2

Sharp as a Sword

Although not used anymore in battle, the sword used to be the main weapon of engagement. Swords were developed back in the Iron Age, around the twelfth century BC. A sword is a fascinating weapon. Forged of steel, the power that it has is largely dependent on the person handling it. The trigger of a gun is simple to pull, but wielding a sword?

Questions and Suggestions

• Read James 3:18. What do you think this verse means? How have you seen this come to pass in your own life experience? Do you know any people of peace? How do they impact your life?
• Pray that God will send people of peace into your life—and that he will also give you such peace.

NOTES

To effectively use a sword requires great skill. A sword is sharp; its blade can be flat and heavy. When a wound is inflicted with a sword, there is a sign. The skin is sliced, blood flows, and the body hurts. Words can be just as sharp as a sword, but there may be no immediate sign of their effect. Words may pierce the heart, numb the mind, and cause long-lasting damage, but the hearer may just bat his or her eyelids and seem unaffected. Those who speak should carefully weigh their words.

Questions and Suggestions

• Read Proverbs 13:3 and Proverbs 21:23. Why should people guard their speech? Are *you* careful with what you say? Do you think before you speak and consider how your words may be perceived?

• Pray that God will help you be aware of your speech and how it impacts others.

Day 3
A Word from the Lord

Has anyone ever delivered a word to you and claimed it was from the Lord? How did you feel about it? In Old Testament times many prophets came with a word from the Lord, and the people ignored their warnings. The prophets made them uncomfortable—probably because their words stirred the people deeply and convicted their hearts. Many dismissed the words that were from the Lord, and as a result were lost to sin. Be willing to open your ears and your heart to hear what God has to say to you—even through the mouth of another person. Be ready to be challenged and grow in God.

Questions and Suggestions

• Are you open to allowing believers to advise you and confront you about sin in your life or about areas where you need to grow? Who would you be willing to hear such words from?

• Pray, asking God to help you accept correction that comes from him.

Day 4
On Guard

Not everyone who speaks to us and claims to share God's wisdom will be speaking from the Lord. How can you tell if their words are legitimate? What advice does the Bible give? In 2 Peter, we are warned to be on guard against false teachers. How can we be on guard? The best way to weigh the words of others is to pray about the advice and see how the Holy Spirit leads us. Godly words will never contradict the Bible. This always provides a measure by which we can assess the legitimacy of the words. We must always be on our guard and full of discernment.

Questions and Suggestions

• What kind of people are "false teachers?" Read 2 Peter 2 in order to learn more about them and what we should do about them.

• Pray that God will give you a spirit to discern when others are speaking on his authority—and always check what is said against the Word!

Day 5
The Result of Peace

The quiet stream flows over the rocks, trickling down the ridge. The grasses whisper softly in the breeze. The green grass carpet is dotted with tiny purple flowers. This carpet continues over rolling hills as far as the eye can see. Above the hills is a brilliant blue sky, scattered with patchy white clouds. It is quiet and still—a picture of peace. This peace begs you to come and relax and enjoy. It implores you to put everything aside and just stop and rest. It wants you to soak up the beauty of creation until it spills from your pores. When you stop and do that, your spirit is refreshed. Your mind thinks good and holy thoughts. Have you met people who are always peaceful to the core? It is because they commune with God, and he daily refreshes their souls. These people bring out goodness in themselves and in others. When you are with them it is quiet and still, and you are encouraged toward holiness.

Leading into the Session

Warm Up

Option 1   Play a tape game.
LITTLE PREP   *Duct tape*

Option 2   Play Steal the Bacon.
MORE PREP   *A messy item for the "bacon," cleaning supplies, candy or other small prizes*

Starting Line

Option 1   Discuss things that separate us from God.
YOUNGER YOUTH   *Premade signs, paper strips, tape, marker*

Option 2   Discuss envy and its impact on relationships.
OLDER YOUTH   *Green robe, hat, and/or face paint, and wet wipes (optional)*

Leading through the Session

Straight Away

Explore the Bible passage.
Bibles

The Turn

Discuss the need for submission to God.
Bibles

Leading beyond the Session

Home Stretch

Option 1   Participate in a time of self-reflection.
YOUNGER YOUTH   *Reproducible 1, pens or pencils; worship music (optional)*

Option 2   Participate in a ritual of washing.
OLDER YOUTH   *Bibles, pitcher of water, bowl, towels; worship music (optional)*

Finish Line

Option 1   Consider how people can submit to God.
LITTLE PREP   *Reproducible 2, pens or pencils*

Option 2   Demonstrate the act of submitting to God.
MORE PREP   *Helium balloons on strings, permanent markers (not fine point)*

SESSION 4

SUBMITTING TO GOD

Bible Passage
James 4:1–12

Key Verses
Submit yourselves, then, to God. Come near to God and he will come near to you.
—James 4:7–8, NRSV

Main Thought
God wants us to submit our lives to him.

157

Bible Background

The marriage covenant is a powerful and enduring biblical metaphor for the relationship between God and his people, whether Israel in the Old Testament or the church in the New. Prophets such as Isaiah, Jeremiah, and above all Hosea portrayed Israel as a faithless spouse, and James took up the same theme in chapter 4. He addressed his readers as "adulterous people"; this is the church, remember, to whom he was writing and of whom he used such harsh language. These were not heathens, but Christians who were having trouble remembering their first love.

The first and second commandments in the Decalogue frame the relationship between the Lord God and his people. The marriage metaphor draws on both. Israel was to have no other gods before God and they were to fashion no idols for, as God declared, "I, the LORD your God, am a jealous God." Idolatry was a persistent problem in Israel's life. It is a demanding religion that calls us to faith in the God who cannot be seen; Canaanite idols were ever-present physical temptations to lapse into a more concrete religion. The situation of the first-century church was not much improved. Gentiles converted to Christianity out of the world of pagan idolatry. Temples and statues of Greco-Roman gods and goddesses called recent converts to return to familiar and more certain ways. None of this excused faithlessness, for Israel and the church are married to a jealous partner who accepts no nonsense when it comes to the seductions of religious rivals: "I am the LORD, your God."

James thought that "the world" also tempts believers away from their first love. The world is a larger and perhaps more seductive rival than false religions. "The world" would seem to include anything not related to God. That encompasses a wide territory. Does our jealous God insist that we have nothing to do with culture—no music other than hymns and no entertainment that lacks a religious theme? Some Christians have understood that their allegiance to Christ demanded such exclusions. The ancient Christian theologian Augustine was converted in part through the earlier conversion of his friend Alypius. As a pagan Alypius had loved attending the arena; forsaking that love for God was part of his decision to become a Christian. In other words, Alypius read James's warning about friendship with the world both broadly and literally.

Are Christians then literally to have nothing to do with the world? This seems an impossible demand. We each have to earn a living, but not all of us can work in Christian schools or Christian bookstores. Perhaps the key here is in the word *friendship*. James warns us against becoming friends with the world. Friendship is a matter of preference. When we prefer the world to the company of God we become divided selves, even to the point where we ask God for what is unworthy of our faith. Work in the world; enjoy the beautiful, inspiring, and yes, even entertaining creations of human culture. But do not ever prefer these over a jealous marriage partner.

Warm Up

OPTION 1 (LITTLE PREP)

Play a tape game.

Use duct tape to mark off an area on the floor about ten by ten feet. You can adjust this based on the number of students in the class. The students need enough room to move around, but not so much that they can stay far away from one another. Give each student a two-inch piece of duct tape. They may place their piece of tape anywhere on themselves but may not hide it under their clothing. Once the tape is in place they may not move it. When all the students have tape on themselves, ask them to step inside the playing box. They have to stay within its borders. At your signal, they will try to steal as many pieces of tape off others as possible while protecting their own piece of tape. If a student has his or her tape stolen, this person has to move outside of the playing area and may not try to steal any more tape. Play for a minute or so, then see which person has the most strips of tape.

Say, **It's hard to flee from someone when you can't step outside the box!**

> **Note:**
> If you sent the Portable Sanctuary home with students last week, take some time at the beginning of this session to review and discuss their experience.

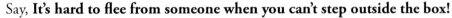

OPTION 2 (MORE PREP)

Play Steal the Bacon.

This game is best played in a large field or yard. It can also be played on a gymnasium floor. Divide the students into two equal teams and have the teams line up across from one another, facing each other. The members of each team should be numbered consecutively. The "bacon" (the object to be stolen) is placed directly in the center between the two teams. Any small, solid object (such as a baseball, an eraser, a book, and so forth) will work for the "bacon"; however, the game is more fun if you use something messy for the "bacon" (actual bacon, an egg, a hamburger, and so forth). The teams should be about ten feet from the bacon. Here's how the setup would look:

1st team	Leader	2nd team
1		6
2		5
3		4
4	Bacon	3
5		2
6		1

The leader calls out a number. The students who are designated with that number race to the center to "steal the bacon." The point of the game is to steal the bacon and race it back to their team. If one team grabs the bacon first, the opposing team is free to try to get it away from that person before he or she reaches "home." (This can be done nonviolently by just tagging the person with the bacon.)

159

If this person makes it "home," he or she will be safe and will have won that round. Make sure you have cleaning supplies ready if necessary. After playing a few rounds, give candy or other small prizes to the team that wins the most rounds.

Say, **It gets our adrenaline going when someone tries to steal something from us.**

Starting Line

OPTION 1 (YOUNGER YOUTH)
Discuss things that separate us from God.
Post on the wall a sign that reads *God* and close to it another sign that reads *You.* Explain that this is a visual demonstration of a relationship where a person is in close fellowship with God. God always loves us and cares for us, but there are things that push us away from having a right relationship with God. Ask, **What kinds of things hinder one's relationship with God?** As students mention some, write them on strips of paper and post the strips between the *God* and *You* signs, moving them farther apart as more strips are added. After several things have been mentioned, ask, **What can a person do to draw closer to God?** As we remove or resolve the issues that separate us from God, the gap can be closed. Remove some of the strips of paper and move the *God* and *You* signs closer again.

When you are ready to move on, say, **Let's see how we can submit ourselves to God and draw near to him.**

* *

Note:

If you use face paint, provide wet wipes so students can clean up.

OPTION 2 (OLDER YOUTH)
Discuss envy and its impact on relationships.
Invite the students to sit in a circle. Ask, **What does it mean to be *envious*? How does it *feel* to be envious? What impact does envy have on the person who is envious?** Envy is a part of our sinful nature—and all of us deal with it in some way. Place a chair or a stool in the center of the circle. Ask students if they have ever heard the phrase "Green with envy." Ask if they are familiar with where the expression came from. You can do some additional research on this phrase, but its roots go at least as far back as Shakespeare. Shakespeare's writings described envy as a green-eyed monster, so since that time people who are intensely envious are described as being green. Invite the students to take turns sitting in the center chair. If possible, furnish a green robe and hat for the person in the chair to put on; give this person green face paint. He or she should use the paint to make a mark on the left cheek while saying, "I am green with envy…" and a mark on the right check while finishing the statement, "…for _____". Students will take turns sharing envious thoughts or feelings that they have. (If you don't have the green robe, hat, and paint, students can still sit in the chair and share their envy statements.) When everyone has had a turn in the chair, point out that envy is the source of many of our conflicts and problems with one another.

When you are ready to move on, say, **Let's see what the Bible says about dealing with envy.**

160

Explore the Bible passage.

Read together James 4:1–12 and discuss the following questions:

- **What source of fighting and quarreling did James focus on here?** Our envy—our desires to have what we can't get. James said that these desires battle within us. We might not want to feel this way, but envy rears its head and sometimes gets the better of us.

- **Do people really *kill* in an attempt to get what they want?** Sure they do! Most of the conflicts and battles around the world are attempts by people to get or keep something, usually political power or land. Some leaders and other people kill citizens of their own countries and even members of their own families in order to get or maintain power and possessions.

- **All this conflict happens over things we want. Why did James say that people do not have what they want?** Because they don't ask God, the one who could truly provide it. Or when they do ask God, their motives are selfish—and God doesn't grant the request. Ask students to talk about some things that people covet and selfishly desire. At times our prayers tend to focus on satisfying our own wants instead of seeking God's plan.

- **Why did James call the people adulterous?** Adultery occurs when someone who is married is unfaithful. Sometimes we put other things before God, letting those things take God's place in our hearts. God loves us intimately, as a spouse would, and when we are unfaithful to him it's like adultery. The people of Israel turned their backs on God time and time again to worship other gods, even though the first of the Ten Commandments is, "You shall have no other gods before me" (Exodus 20:3). People also worship other gods today, when they put other things before God.

- **How did James contrast our approach to God and our approach to the devil?** We should submit to God (give in to his will) and resist the devil, who will flee from us. Point out that people often get these actions reversed—they submit to the things the devil tempts them to do and resist the Spirit of God urging them to stay away from sin.

- **James encouraged us to come near to God. What other actions come along with this?** When we come near to God, he will come near to us. God does not force himself upon us; he makes the offer and waits for us to respond. Those who come near the holy God must wash and purify themselves, mourning because of their sinfulness. The guilt of our sin should pierce our hearts completely! But when we humble ourselves before God in this way, God will lift us up.

- **What is slander—and what are you doing when you slander someone?** Slander is speaking falsely against another person, saying something about that person that is not true. When we do this we are judging that person.

- **What will happen if we judge others? Whose task is it?** If we judge others, then we are judging the law itself. God is the one who gives the law, so he is the one who should judge.

Say, **God invites us to submit ourselves to him.**

The Turn

Discuss the need for submission to God.

Invite a student to read Acts 17:26–27. Ask, **Why were we created?** God created us to be in relationship with him. However, as you discussed earlier, this relationship will not be forced on us. It is up to us to decide whether or not we want to walk with God. God is nearby, ready to be in relationship with us. Invite a student to read Psalm 145:18, which also reinforces this truth. Invite the students to share how it feels to know that God created us to be in relationship with him and is always willing to draw near to us. In order to have a relationship with God, we need to understand the position he should have in our lives. When we *submit* to someone, we let that person be in control. When the students submit to their parents, elders, or teachers they are accepting the parameters that those people set. They are agreeing to let the wisdom of those people guide them.

Invite a student to read Hebrews 12:9–10. Ask, **Why does this say we should submit to God?** Because God knows what is best for us. By submitting to God, we may live. Remind the students that Christ modeled submission through his life. Such submission is illustrated in the Lord's Prayer (Matthew 6:9–13). Jesus taught us to pray that God's will be done on earth as it is in heaven. Christ also demonstrated submission at the painful end of his life. Ask a student to read Matthew 26:39. Jesus did not *want* to endure the suffering, but he put his own will aside, even when he had full awareness of the physical pain and the pain of separation from the father that he would face.

Say, **Christ put his trust in God's divine purposes. God is asking *us* to place that same kind of trust in him.**

Home Stretch

OPTION 1 (YOUNGER YOUTH)

Participate in a time of self-reflection.

Distribute to the students copies of "Our Golden Calves" (Reproducible 1) and provide time for the class to thoughtfully and prayerfully respond to the questions. (You may wish to play some worship music in the background during this time, particularly songs that have to do with confession or purifying and cleansing our hearts.) If time permits, invite the students to share some of their thoughts. Encourage anyone dealing with a particularly painful or urgent issue to speak with you after class.

When you are ready to move on, say, **Today God invites you to put other things aside and draw near to him.**

OPTION 2 (OLDER YOUTH)

Participate in a ritual of washing.

At the side of the room prepare a table with a pitcher of water, a bowl, and towels. Direct the students to focus on this activity by reading James 4:6 and Psalm 51:10. Provide time for silent reflection, during which the students can ask God to reveal to them areas of sinfulness in their lives. (You may wish to play some worship music in the background during this time, particularly songs that have to do with confession or purifying and cleansing our hearts.) Encourage them to ask God about anything they have placed before him in their lives, and to think about whether or not they struggle with submitting completely to God. Encourage students to take turns during this time pouring water over their hands at the side of the room. This will signify that they are confessing their sinfulness to God. If some students are still working on issues with God and are not at a point where they feel as if they can participate in the washing, they should not feel pressured to do so. Say, **Be honest with yourself and with God about where you're at today.** Encourage anyone dealing with a particularly painful or urgent issue to speak with you after class.

When you are ready to move on, say, **Today God invites you purify your heart and draw near to him.**

Finish Line

OPTION 1 (LITTLE PREP)

Consider how people can submit to God.

Invite the students to form groups of three or four and to read and respond to the situations found in "Living Submitted" (Reproducible 2). (This reproducible is also available on the Digital BRIDGES CD as a projection.) After the groups have had time to work on the situations, invite them to share their responses with the rest of the class. Encourage your students for their efforts to apply what they have learned about submitting ourselves to God.

Close the session by praying that God will help your students to submit to him daily in their lives.

. . . .

OPTION 2 (MORE PREP)

Demonstrate the act of submitting to God.

Give each student a colored helium balloon on a string. Furnish permanent markers (not fine point) for the students to use to decorate their balloons with a large sign of a cross. As a group, take your balloons outside and stand in a circle. Ask, **What do you need to do in order to submit your life fully to God?** As a students shares, he or she should release the balloon into the sky. This will be a symbol for your students of releasing their lives to the Lord. After everyone has taken a turn, join hands and close in prayer, asking God to help your students submit to him daily in their lives. If weather permits, you might ask the students to kneel for this prayer as a further demonstration of submission to God.

Note:

Don't forget to distribute copies of the Portable Sanctuary to students before they go.

Where Young Adults Find Direction for Life

Young adults are at different places in life, seeking answers to difficult questions. They don't want to hear lectures or memorize neat little formulas. They want to find direction in life, having the support of a community of faith yet the freedom to explore.

The Journey is a discipleship resource to help young adults along the journey of life and faith. It's a postmodern resource—an extended conversation about discipleship. *The Journey* is designed to help young adults *discover* authentic relationships, *develop* a mutually supportive community, and be *deployed* for practical outreach and service. To get a taste of *the Journey*, go to...

www.thejourneynet.org

You'll step into a fascinating world of faith exploration where you will find Internet links to Scripture, commentaries, music, artwork, history, and other resources for the life of Christian discipleship.

The Journey is not a teacher's guide or a set of lecture notes. It is not designed to be completed in a certain amount of time. A visitor to this site can use the resources as needed, in the order they're needed, and can revisit the site as often as desired.

- -

CHURCH *of* GOD MINISTRIES

HOW TO BEGIN

It's easy to begin to *the Journey*. Just go online and navigate to this website:

www.thejourneynet.org

You'll have instant access to the resources you need for your spiritual journey.

If you encounter any problems with login or registration, please contact our webmanager via e-mail at webticket@chog.org.

Journey www.thejourneynet.org

Our Golden Calves

Not long after God miraculously rescued his people from Egypt and provided for them, the people seemed to forget about their relationship with God. They created an idol of gold in the form of a calf. They bowed down to this idol and worshiped it, giving it God's place in their hearts (Exodus 32).

In the chart above, describe with words or picture some things or people that you tend to put in God's place. Consider the things you have written or drawn. Are these things effective? Have they satisfied you? Have they met your expectations?

Next to each thing on the chart, write the main drawback of that thing or person. How does it fail to satisfy?

What keeps you from fully submitting to God and putting him first? How can you reprioritize your life and put God first?

_____

_____

Living Submitted

Read and discuss the following situations with your group; then share your ideas with the rest of the class after everyone is finished.

Situation 1

Malory always felt that she was destined for something amazing. When she was a young teen she felt that God wanted her to be in some kind of ministry. Her mind had reeled with the possibilities—missionary to some distant foreign land, ministry to children or youth—the possibilities seemed endless and exciting. But that was long ago. Now she is not sure if that was God directing—maybe it was just an emotional adventure at summer church camp. Now she feels that she's facing "reality." Her parents are struggling to keep their business going and have told Malory that they really need her help. Is this what God wants for her? How can Malory submit to God in this situation? What do you recommend she do and why?

Situation 2

The new student in Marcus's class really seems unsure of himself. His awkwardness is obvious and he has already become the brunt of many jokes. Although Marcus laughs when his friends joke about this new student, deep inside he just doesn't feel right about it. On a few occasions Marcus has greeted the new student, who has quickly looked away as if he were embarrassed and did not want to be noticed. A week from now the school is having a tailgate party after the football game. Ever since his girlfriend suggested that he invite the new student to join them, Marcus can't get it out of his mind. But wouldn't that be crazy? How would the other students react? Would an invitation like that make it worse or better for the new student? How can Marcus submit to God in this situation? What do you recommend he do and why?

Situation 3

Lauryn has been dating Shawn for over a year. They've been one of the most popular couples in school. For the past few weeks Shawn has been acting distant and disturbed, so Lauryn tried to find out what was bothering him. He was not immediately forthcoming, but Lauryn finally learned that he wants to break up with her. Lauryn believes that they are still supposed to be together, and is disappointed that Shawn says he's not interested in a relationship anymore. He still seems to care for her, and that's confusing. She's not sure if she should let him go or fight for their relationship. How can Lauryn submit to God in this matter? What do you recommend she do and why?

Portable Sanctuary

Day 1

Complete Submission

It can't be this way, his mind screamed. The dark of the night crushed him as he saw the whips come crashing down. Inwardly he groaned as he saw the nails being placed on his wrist and felt them pierce muscle and shatter bone. Their intense hatred overwhelmed his soul. *I don't think I can bear this.* His heart was further crushed by the glimpse of his mother's face and the grief and bewilderment on the faces of his disciples. *They don't understand. Oh God, if it is possible, may this cup be taken from me ... yet ... not as I will, but as you will.*

Questions and Suggestions

• How does the model of Christ's submission encourage you?
• Mediate on what Christ did for you when he took your place on the cross. Thank him for his sacrifice and for his obedience to the Father. Ask him to help you follow his example.

Day 2

Security Blanket No More

The cartoon character Linus is perhaps the most famous blanket carrier of all time. Little kids often use blankets to console themselves as they get used to being separated from their parents. A blanket is warm and snuggly and helps them feel that they are not alone. However, when they are back in the company of their parents or are in the midst of exciting play you might see the blanket lying on the floor in the corner. We often treat our relationship with God the same way. When we are hurting or in need, we call on God to draw near to us. We call for God's help, intervention, and presence in our lives. When things are better, our relationship is dropped in the corner and forgotten until the next trial. We should be more like Linus, who carries his blanket wherever he goes—even in the middle of a baseball game! God should always be in the forefront of our minds.

Questions and Suggestions
• Is it easy for you to discard your relationship with God when things are going well and you are comfortable? Why or why not?
• Ask God to help bring your relationship with him to mind even when things are going well.

Day 3
A Jealous God

God loves you so much. God is your Creator—he formed you with his hands and breathed the breath of life into you. God's greatest desire is to be in relationship with you. Song of Songs 4:9 says that you have stolen God's heart. God's love for you was so great that God even sent his only Son to redeem you with his blood (John 3:16). God's heart is stirred to jealousy when your love is given to other things or people and you turn your back on God. Exodus 34:14 says, "Do not worship any other god, for the LORD, whose name is Jealous, is a jealous God." God's love for you is deep and abiding—and he desires that in return.

Questions and Suggestions
• How does it impact you to know how much God loves you? How should you respond to that love? How does it impact you to know that God is jealous of your affections? What do you give your heart to instead of God?
• Spend some time opening your heart to God.

Day 4
Heart Surgery

With fluid movements and extraordinary skill his hands move, wielding instruments with great care. Cuts are made precisely, opening valves and repairing arteries. Blood is diverted and things are transplanted. God is the master heart surgeon. God knows which things should not be occupying our hearts, and as we submit ourselves to God's art, he cuts those things away. It is painful and grieving, but as the process continues our hearts are reshaped into something new and beautiful. God's work continues, bringing us closer to whom God wants us to be.

Questions and Suggestions
• Read Philippians 1:6. For this kind of change to occur in our hearts, what has to happen first?
• Have you been letting God work in your heart? What has God been showing to you? Pray about it.

Day 5
We Are Nothing

The proud are confident of their abilities. They are so sure of themselves that they feel they can do or be without God. The proud have a warped sense of self, for they do not see that we are truly nothing. God wants us to have a realistic view of who we are and to recognize that we are nothing without him. When we get ourselves in proper perspective, then God will be able to use us and change us. Remember, he doesn't force his way in. He patiently knocks and waits at the door (Revelation 3:20).

Questions and Suggestions
• Read Psalm 25:8–10. What is the Lord like? How does God interact with people? How do you see yourself in these verses?
• Write a poem or a free verse describing God's interaction with you.

Leading into the Session

Warm Up

Option 1
LITTLE PREP
Discuss situations where prayer might help.
Reproducible 1, pens or pencils

Option 2
MORE PREP
Discuss how feelings are expressed.
Happy, Sad, Angry, and Concerned/Fearful signs and accompanying decorations

Starting Line

Option 1
YOUNGER YOUTH
Unscramble and define the word *prayer.*
Large cutout letters P-R-A-Y-E-R

Option 2
OLDER YOUTH
Discuss different types of prayer.
Bibles, copies of different types of prayers, tape, paper, pens or pencils

Leading through the Session

Straight Away

Explore the Bible passage.
Bibles

The Turn

Discuss the characteristics of prayer warriors.
Bibles, chalkboard or dry erase board

Leading beyond the Session

Home Stretch

Option 1
YOUNGER YOUTH
Write an ACTS prayer.
Reproducible 2, pens or pencils

Option 2
OLDER YOUTH
Share prayer concerns from the heart.

Finish Line

Option 1
LITTLE PREP
Covenant to pray for one another.

Option 2
MORE PREP
Participate in a prayer meeting.
Time, transportation, and arrangements necessary to attend a prayer or healing service

---

SESSION 5

HOLD ON!

Bible Passage
James 5

Key Verse
Pray for each other.... The prayer of a righteous [person] is powerful and effective.
—James 5:16

Main Thought
Prayer is an important part of our spiritual lives.

Bible Background

The body is a powerful biblical image, particularly in the New Testament. As has often been noted, ancient peoples throughout the Mediterranean world assumed that human beings were naturally social creatures for whom life in society logically and naturally preceded their individual existence. In other words, an individual man or woman was an extension of the whole body politic. Paul really meant it when he said that in the body of Christ, the church, the suffering of one member is the suffering of all, and the joy of one is also shared by all. James also thought of the church in the metaphor of the body, and his advice to those who are sick should be interpreted against that backdrop.

Just as singing comes naturally to the happy, or prayer to the needy and troubled, a sick person's immediate reflex should be to call the church and the church leaders. This is the body working to bring healing and restoration to one of its members. Just as white blood cells gather from throughout a physical body at the site of an infection, so believers are to gather around an afflicted brother or sister. There is no medicine like the physical presence of church members gathering to console, to pray, to embrace, and to anoint. Countless numbers of believers can testify to God's healing touch conveyed through the fingers and arms of church people.

The medical arts and sciences have been radically transformed since the time James wrote his instructions to sick Christians. Not much more than a century ago medical practice was still fairly primitive by today's standards. The story is told of the elder Doctor Mayo calling one of his sons, later founders of the renowned clinic that bears the family name, for emergency assistance in a surgery. No more than junior high age, the boy was needed to administer anesthesia, but he was so short that he had to stand on an overturned cracker box to reach the patient. Small wonder that many nineteenth- and early twentieth-century Americans were skeptical of doctors and medicine. We have become so accustomed to the wondrous techniques and tools of modern medicine that coronary bypass surgery has become commonplace for all but the patient and his or her family. In such a world it is not to be wondered that when illness strikes our first recourse is often to physicians and nurses rather than the church.

There once was a time when some believers thought that they must choose between mutually exclusive alternatives. They believed that they could trust only one healer—either God or medical science. Faith in one automatically cancelled the possible recourse to the other. It still should be a basic Christian instinct to call the church when someone becomes seriously ill. The body wants to send healing agents where it hurts. But trust in God can and does cooperate with physicians and nurses. It's one of the principle reasons the church has sent medical missionaries to some of the world's neediest countries. We might think of these men and women as the body of Christ's specialized healing agents sent to some of its most afflicted members.

OPTION 1 (LITTLE PREP)

Discuss situations where prayer might help.

Distribute copies of "Looking for Help" (Reproducible 1) or show it as a projection, ask the students to pair up, and encourage them to read and respond to the situations in the handout. After a few minutes, invite those who are willing to share their responses with the rest of the class.

Say, **For many people, prayer is an important part of their lives.**

Warm Up

· ·

OPTION 2 (MORE PREP)

Discuss how feelings are expressed.

Prior to class, select four separate areas of the room. Label and decorate each according to the following suggestions:

> *Note:*
> If you sent the Portable Sanctuary home with students last week, take some time at the beginning of this session to review and discuss their experience.

- *Happy*—brightly-colored balloons and crepe paper, pictures of sunshine and people laughing, beanbag chairs
- *Sad*—black crepe paper, pictures of sorrowful people and bleak landscapes, a box of tissues, single chairs spaced away from one another
- *Angry*—red crepe paper, pictures of people yelling or in conflict, punching bag and boxing gloves (if possible), no chairs
- *Concerned/Fearful*—all different colors of crepe paper, strange and confusing pictures, decorations that give a sense of chaos

When the students enter the room, ask them to go to the area for an emotion they have recently experienced. Ideally you will have students in all four areas; if an area has only one person in it, ask another student to join that area. Ask the students to discuss with those in their area why they felt that emotion recently. Whenever they feel this way, how do they usually express it? Each person in the group should answer these questions.

After a few minutes, ask the groups to switch areas (perhaps by rotating clockwise). In their new areas they should discuss what might bring this emotion to the surface in their lives, and how they usually express this emotion. Rotate two more times so that everyone has talked about each emotion in the room.

When the students are finished, discuss this activity by utilizing the following questions:

- **What area did you like the most?**
- **Which emotion do you experience most often in your life?**
- **Were you surprised by the way the other people in your group expressed their emotions?**
- **Did you all express emotions similarly, or were your expressions different?**
- **Do you think that people of different cultures express emotions differently?**

Say, **It would be nice to be happy all the time, but we all experience a variety of emotions.**

Starting Line

OPTION 1 (YOUNGER YOUTH)
Unscramble and define the word **prayer.**

Place large letters that spell *P-R-A-Y-E-R* all around the room. Do not hide them behind or inside things, but do not necessarily make them easy to see. Do not put the letters in order, but scramble them. Ask students to find the word in the room and unscramble it. When they have done this, ask them to describe prayer. (If you have a large class, make several sets of letters in different colors. The first team to find and unscramble the word in their designated color would win. Members of each group could then discuss their personal descriptions of prayer.)

When you are ready to move on, say, **Let's look at some different situations that call for prayer.**

· ·

OPTION 2 (OLDER YOUTH)
Discuss different types of prayer.

Prepare printouts of different types of prayers and post them around the room (e.g., a prayer of confession, a prayer for healing, a prayer of thanksgiving, a prayer of supplication, and so forth). Do not label which type of prayer is which. Furnish paper and pens or pencils and invite the students to walk around the room, reading the prayers and attempting to identify each type. After a few minutes, discuss the types of prayer you have posted. Help the students better understand any types they were not familiar with.

Ask, **Did you know that in the Bible there are actually different labels for prayers?** Invite students to look at the Book of Psalms and see if they can find the different types of prayers within David's writings.

When you are ready to move on, say, **Let's see what the Book of James says about prayer.**

Straight Away

Explore the Bible passage.

Read together James 5:1–20 and discuss the following questions:

- **How can unpaid wages "cry out"?** This refers to a deed or a fact being noticed by someone. When Cain murdered Abel, God said that Abel's blood had cried out from the ground (Genesis 4:10). In this case, God has heard the cries of the people who were oppressed by the rich—and the rich will have to reckon with God.
- **What examples of patience did James give?** Farmers are patient with their crops, planting and then waiting for months for the rains and then the harvest. The prophets patiently continued to deliver the word of the Lord, even when the people didn't accept it and it seemed that God would never make things right. Job was patient and persistent in his faith in God, even when he tragically lost his family and his possessions.
- **What circumstances call for us to turn to God, either in prayer or**

praise? When we are in trouble, when we are happy, and when we are sick. Point out that this is not intended to be an exhaustive list; the point is, we should talk to God no matter *what* is going on in our lives.

- **What further instructions did James give for when we are sick?** We should call the elders (church leaders) to come and pray for us and anoint us with oil. Explain that oil was used often in Bible times. In worship it was a sign of consecration or setting something apart for special use. (If time permits, you can look at Exodus 30:22–33.)

- **According to this text, what will happen when a prayer is offered in faith?** The person will be healed and raised up by God, and his or her sins forgiven. Discuss honestly with your students the fact that sometimes we pray with much faith but a person is not made well. How do these situations challenge their faith in the promises of God? Some people say, "The issue must be with us—we need to have *more* faith," or, "Going to heaven is the *ultimate* healing." This may be true, but it is not necessarily the sense of the text. There are no easy answers. It's beyond us to see God's purposes or understand all of God's ways. The reality is that we have seen God miraculously heal in this world. We have seen God answer the prayers of the faithful. For that reason we trust and we pray with faith in every situation.

- **Whenever we see "therefore" in the biblical text, we should consider what it's there for. In this case, what did James call on believers to do?** We should confess our sins to one another and pray for one another so that we may be healed; there is great power in this kind of prayer. The idea is *frequent, consistent* confession and prayer. If sin comes into our lives, we should confess it and get it out of the way as soon as possible, and we should pray about all things. This is the basis for accountability partners and groups. There are Christians who meet with a trusted partner or group where they confess their sins to one another and pray for one another. These are persons who can frankly ask about our hearts and our relationship with God. Encourage your students to think about whether they would like to develop that kind of transparent relationship with someone as a way to experience continued spiritual growth.

- **Why did James bring up the story of Elijah?** See 1 Kings 17—18. Elijah was just a man, but by his prayer God stopped the rain for about three years. This is an example of an incredibly effective prayer!

- **How can bringing someone back to spiritual truth save that person from death and cover over his or her sins? Isn't that God's job?** Our only hope for eternal life is in God. If we help someone who has strayed from God come back to God, then that person has entered the path of life again. As a part of that returning, the person will repent and seek forgiveness for sin; this person's future sins will also be averted. Point out that it is important for us to help people find the truth so they will not perish.

Say, **According to James, prayer brings forgiveness and healing—and can even save lives!**

The Turn

Discuss the characteristics of prayer warriors.

Ask, **Have you heard the term "prayer warrior"? What does this refer to?** This refers to someone who is as committed to and serious about prayer as a soldier, doing battle with the forces of evil by staying on his or her knees before God. Invite the students to think of particular individuals they would identify as prayer warriors. What kind of characteristics have they witnessed in these people's lives? What makes these people qualify as prayer warriors? As the students share characteristics, write them on the board.

Explain that one characteristic of a prayer warrior should be steadfast faith, since faith is at the core of prayer. Invite a student to read Matthew 21:22. Ask, **According to Christ, how will we receive what we ask for in prayer?** By believing, or having faith. As established earlier, not every prayer we say with faith is answered. Some prayers are not answered because of sin present in the life of the believer (see Psalm 66:18–19). Sometimes the answer *we* hope for is not within God's plan or purpose; our expectations do not fit into God's design. As you studied last week, we need to be willing to submit ourselves to God's plan and not demand our own way.

Invite a student to read 2 Corinthians 12:7–10 and discuss the following questions:

- **What was plaguing Paul?** A thorn in the flesh, from Satan. Scholars have debated whether this was a literal thorn or some other kind of ailment that continued to plague Paul.
- **What did Paul do about it?** Paul prayed three times for God to remove it. Remind the students that Paul was indeed a man of faith. He probably also felt that his ministry could be more effective without this "thorn in the flesh." Yet despite his faithful petition, God did not answer in the way Paul had hoped.
- **How *did* God answer?** That God's grace was sufficient for Paul, and that God's power would be shown in Paul's weakness. This weakness was to bring glory to God.
- **What was Paul's conclusion about the problem of unanswered prayer?** He welcomed it, knowing that God can be strong in those areas and be glorified. Sometimes we are able to understand why our prayers are not answered and sometimes we don't understand, but we need to remain steadfast in the faith.

Invite a student to read 1 John 3:21–22. Ask, **How can we be confident before God and be certain that our prayers will be answered?** By making sure we are righteous and our hearts are not sinful, and by obeying God's commands and doing what pleases him.

Invite a student to read Psalm 34:15, 17. Ask, **Whom is the Lord watching and listening to, and what does God do for them?** God watches over and listens to the righteous; he hears and delivers them.

Say, **You can become a powerful and effective prayer warrior if you have a firm faith and a righteous life.**

OPTION 1 (YOUNGER YOUTH)

Write an ACTS prayer.

Explain to students that a single prayer can have several different parts. One model we can use in our prayers is the ACTS model—*A*doration, *C*onfession, *T*hanksgiving, and *S*upplication. Define these terms for students as follows:

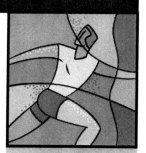

Home Stretch

> *A*doration—Worshiping and adoring God for who he is, for his nature (loving, compassionate, patient, steadfast, and so forth)
>
> *C*onfession—Telling God things you have done wrong, getting them off your chest and asking forgiveness for them
>
> *T*hanksgiving—Thanking God for the good things he has done in your life (family, friends, health, a home, and so forth)
>
> *S*upplication—Taking your needs and the needs of others to God (healing, salvation, employment, relationship issues, and so forth)

Distribute copies of "The Lord's Prayer: ACTS" (Reproducible 2); invite the students to examine the Lord's Prayer and determine what each statement is—adoration, confession, thanksgiving, or supplication—and why. When they are finished, review their results. Ask, **Do you think prayer should *always* have these components?** Regardless of the form we use, it is good to have some overall balance to our prayers—including times of listening for God's response! Invite the students to spend a few minutes composing their own prayers following the ACTS model. Encourage them to keep their prayers in a journal, and challenge them to add other prayers to the journal.

When you are ready to move on, say, **Including different elements in our prayers can bring great power and have dramatic effects.**

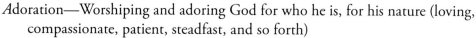

OPTION 2 (OLDER YOUTH)

Share prayer concerns from the heart.

Invite the students to examine their hearts and each think of one issue they are dealing with that they are comfortable sharing with the rest of the class, and invite other students to say simple prayers for those needs, one at a time. Encourage each student to share at least one need and pray for at least one need. (You might have the students do this in small groups if you have a large class.) Say, **Praying out loud is nothing to be afraid of or embarrassed about, and it doesn't have to be long or fancy.** Laying hands on a person when praying for him or her is appropriate.

When you are ready to move on, say, **God wants us to pray for one another's needs; such prayer is a gift from God, and it works!**

Finish Line

Note:

Don't forget to distribute copies of the Portable Sanctuary to students before they go.

OPTION 1 (LITTLE PREP)

Covenant to pray for one another.

Invite the students to consider if they would like to covenant to pray for one another on a regular basis. Help them think of ways they can share their needs with one another (perhaps on a list that you keep at youth group, by phone chain, or by e-mail). Ask them to also consider whether they would like to share with and pray for everyone in the class, if they would like to split by gender (advisable), or if they would like to choose prayer and accountability partners. Help facilitate discussion on this decision. Regardless of the method chosen, remind the students about the need to maintain confidentiality and not discuss names or requests with others without permission.

Close the session by praying that God will open the eyes of your students to see what happens when they pray as James instructed.

. . . .

OPTION 2 (MORE PREP)

Participate in a prayer meeting.

Find out about a prayer or healing service that you and your students can attend together. (Attending one in a different church may enhance the learning experience for your group.) Communicate the time and location of the service (perhaps with flyers) and make sure you have the necessary arrangements and permission slips to take the students off-site. After attending the service, spend some time in feedback with your students. How did they feel during the service? What did they learn? What types of prayer did they observe? What were the volume, mood, and activity levels like? Did anything seem uncomfortable or out of place? What new things will they now incorporate into their *own* prayer lives?

Close today's session by praying that God will open the eyes of your students to see what happens when they pray as James instructed.

Looking for Help

Situation One

Michael's sister was in an accident last night; she was hit by a drunk driver. The drunk driver walked away from the scene unharmed but Michael's sister is now fighting for her life. It's completely unfair. Why should Michael's sister be paying for that drunk's mistake? Michael is not allowed to visit his sister yet because she is still in intensive care. As he looks through the glass window at her broken and bruised body, all he feels is anger and pain.

How could prayer help Michael? List all the ways that prayer could help in this particular situation:

_____

_____

_____

Situation Two

Shanti told her best friend something in confidence, but now Shanti has heard other people talking about it. Shanti feels betrayed that her friend shared her secret and is not sure how she can repair the damage to her confidence. She just wants to crawl into a hole and die—and she's pretty sure that she will never trust anyone again.

How could prayer help Shanti? List all the ways that prayer could help in this particular situation:

_____

_____

_____

Situation Three

Ramone was switching channels on the television last night and ended up watching the news. He was assaulted by stories of car bombings, domestic violence, abuse, and drug busts. As he listened he felt a great weight crushing him. *What a disappointment this world is! Nothing good ever seems to happen!*

How could prayer help Ramone? List all the ways that prayer could help in this particular situation:

_____

_____

_____

Situation Four

Kate is still in shock. It's been a while since the pregnancy test came back positive, but she still can't believe it's true. She feels so guilty and ashamed. The fear has been gnawing on her for weeks. Her parents are going to be so angry! How can she even get the words out to tell them what happened and how sorry she is? She is sure that God will never forgive her—and she knows that she can never forgive herself.

How could prayer help Kate? List all the ways that prayer could help in this particular situation:

_____

_____

_____

The Lord's Prayer: ACTS

For each statement of the Lord's Prayer listed below, determine if it is *adoration, confession, thanksgiving,* or *supplication.* If you think it is none of those, write *other.* Write a short reason why you chose each response.

Our Father in heaven, hallowed [respected and honored] be your name.

Type: _____

Why? _____

Your kingdom come, your will be done on earth as it is in heaven.

Type: _____

Why? _____

Give us today our daily bread.

Type: _____

Why? _____

Forgive us our debts, as we also have forgiven our debtors.

Type: _____

Why? _____

And lead us not into temptation, but deliver us from the evil one.

Type: _____

Why? _____

Portable Sanctuary

NOTES

Day 1

The Controversy

Some Christians do not believe in modern medicine. They believe that when illness strikes, they should follow the instructions of the Bible and pray. However, in following the Bible to the letter, they refuse any other intervention. Some of these parents have faced charges because the state saw this "inaction" as neglect or endangerment. Other Christians see medicine as a gift from God and use it as a tool to treat an illness, even as they continue to pray fervently. Must healing prayer and medicine be exclusive?

Questions and Suggestions

- How do you feel about this controversy? What do you believe about faith and medicine?
- Investigate what the Bible says about using medicines or ointments for healing.

Day 2

Praying When?

Five times a day, seven days a week, the loudspeaker blares. It is a reminder to all Muslims, wherever they live in the city, that it is time for prayer. In every neighborhood there are mosques, so not one home can be excused from hearing the call. Even the radio and the television programming are interrupted to call people to prayer. If a Muslim wants to have a better opportunity to reach paradise, he or she had better stop and pray at *every* prescribed time. When should Christians pray? First Chronicles 16:11 says, "Look to the LORD and his strength; seek his face always." First Thessalonians 5:18 echoes this verse, instructing believers to pray continually; There is no time in our day when we should be far from talking to and thinking about God.

Questions and Suggestions

- What does it mean to pray "continually," or "without ceasing"? How often do you think about God and talk to him?
- Try to keep a record one day of your interactions with God. What did this tell you?

Day 3
Meaningless Prayer?

Every day they race to the table for lunch. With their chubby faces bowed and grubby fingers folded they prattle, "Dear Jesus, thank you for this food. Amen!" Every day they say the same words, their speed seemingly related to how hungry their bellies are. Although it's good to teach little children to stop and thank God, they are often not thinking about what they are saying. They're focused on the delicious smell that is wafting off the plate. Do you pray like this sometimes? Have you prayed a prayer without even thinking about your words?

Questions and Suggestions

- What have your prayers been like recently? Have they been dutiful recitations or heartfelt encounters?
- When you pray today, make an effort to choose your words carefully and truly examine your heart's intent.

Day 4
Praying All Night

It was a fairly dark night. Only a bare sliver of the moon hung in the sky like a crooked smile. The stars faintly twinkled. It was still, calm, and quiet. There were the tiniest, hardly discernable noises of insect life but otherwise, dead calm. As he trudged up the mountainside, the occasional loose stone made the most noise. He found an open patch of grassy earth and settled into comfortable conversation with his Father. The conversation lasted until the sun's rays pierced the sky, "One of those days Jesus went out to a mountainside to pray, and spent the night praying to God" (Luke 6:12).

Questions and Suggestions

- Could you pray *all night* on a mountainside? Have you ever done this? How easy it would be to be overcome with the drowsiness of sleep! Many times Jesus went off on his own to pray (Mark 1:35; 6:46; Luke 5:16). What does this say to us?
- Find a solitary place this week to spend some time with God. Spend 25 percent of the time talking, and 75 percent listening to God.

Day 5
Gun Shy

After a few prayers go unanswered we sometimes find ourselves afraid to hope that God will (or even *can*) answer the next one. A series of disappointments can put us in a ditch of despair, a place without trust in the sovereignty of God. It is hard to walk away from those moments with your head held high and your faith intact. It's easier to believe that God just does not care about us than to accept that God will use the situation somehow for his glory. We would rather God fix everything and make it all better. After all, comfort is much more appealing than suffering and pain! What will you do when your prayers keep going unanswered? Will you walk away from God, or will you grab on to your faith all the more tightly and look for God's work unfolding in your life?

Questions and Suggestions

- Read James 1:2–4. Why should we rejoice when we are going through hard times (such as when our prayers go unanswered)? What will the testing of our faith in God produce?
- Next time a prayer of yours goes unanswered, seek to discover what you might learn from the situation.

Leading a Teenager to Christ

Throughout the year, natural times may come up to share the plan of salvation with your students. When that opportunity arises, you will want to be ready with a simple explanation told in a noncoercive manner. You may want to write it out or go over in your mind ahead of time what you will say. Following is a suggested plan and some related scriptures to spark your own prayerful thinking.

Share these thoughts in your own words:

1. God loves you and offers a wonderful plan for your life (John 3:16 and John 10:10).
2. Each of us has sinned and been separated from God, preventing us from knowing and experiencing God's plan (Romans 3:23 and Romans 6:23).
3. Jesus Christ is God's provision for our sin and separation from God (Romans 5:8 and John 14:6).
4. When we place our faith in Jesus Christ as Savior and Lord, then we can know and experience God's love and plan for our lives (John 1:12 and Ephesians 2:8–9).

Receiving Christ involves turning to God from self (repentance) and trusting Christ to come into our lives to forgive our sins and to make us what God wants us to be. It is not enough to agree to a list of facts about Jesus Christ or to have an emotional experience. We receive Jesus Christ by *faith,* as an act of the *will.*

If a student indicates that he or she is ready to make a decision, ask that person if he or she has any questions. If all seems clear, encourage the student to pray a prayer of repentance, asking God's forgiveness. You might guide the student with the following prayer:

God, I know I've done wrong and gone my own way. I am sorry. I want to follow you. I know Jesus died for my sins. I accept Jesus as my Savior and Lord. Thank you for forgiving me. Thank you for the gift of eternal life.

After the student has prayed, thank God for hearing his or her prayer, and affirm the student as a new Christian.

Explain to your student that as we pray, read the Bible, worship with other Christians, and tell others about what God has done for us, God will help us know how to live. Christ's presence is with us to help us live God's way. One step that a new believer should take is to be baptized. Baptism tells others that we are serious about following Jesus. Jesus set the example in being baptized, and we are baptized to show that we are living for Jesus.

Talk to your pastor and your student's parents about his or her decision. Continue to encourage your student by giving him or her instruction and materials for setting up a daily devotional time. If possible, make arrangements with someone in the church to meet regularly with your student to act as a spiritual mentor.

There are a number of simple tract-type visuals to help you share Christ with your students:

- *It's Awesome!* (available at www.warnerpress.org or 800-741-7721)
- *Bridge to Life* (available at www.navpress.org)
- *The Answer* (available at www.studentdiscipleship.org)

BRIDGES for youth

BRIDGES elective studies help teenagers connect the truth of Scripture with the questions they face every day. Their learning activities catch the imagination of junior-high and senior-high youth. Each study has 13 sessions, ideal for three months of weekly studies, or you can tailor a study plan to suit your own calendar.

Life and Leadership

What are the unique challenges of a Christian leader? How do young people respond to natural leaders within their group?

Book 978-1-59317-374-6
Retail $14.99

CD-ROM K30059CD
Retail $24.95

Built to Last

Life has its ups and downs. What should a believer do to stay true to God "on the mountaintop" as well as "in the valley"?

Book 978-1-59317-310-4
Retail $14.99

CD-ROM K10058CD
Retail $24.95

A Journey of Change

As God led the Israelites through the wilderness for forty years, he can lead us through a lifetime of unexpected turns.

Book 978-1-59317-368-5
Retail $14.99

CD-ROM K20059CD
Retail $24.95

Responding to God

God's Holy Spirit can "lead us into all truth" about ourselves—including the truth about our life vocation.

Book 978-1-59317-314-2
Retail $14.99

CD-ROM K40058CD
Retail $24.95

The Savior in Matthew

Jesus calls young people to commit their lives to him, just as he called the first Twelve. How does that calling change our lives?

Book 978-1-59317-375-3
Retail $14.99

CD-ROM K40059CD
Retail $24.95

The Call to Righteousness

God expects his people to live differently than other people do. What kind of holy living does he expect of young people today?

Book 978-1-59317-560-3
Retail $14.99

CD-ROM K20052CD
Retail $24.95

A Community of Eternal Love

What's the most distinctive thing about the church? John's epistles and the book of Revelation give surprising insights.

Book 978-1-59317-306-7
Retail $14.99

CD-ROM K10057CD
Retail $24.95

What Is a Christian?

Our commitment to Christ will be visible and lived out practically. Learn how God changes our lives as we grow in Christ.

Book 978-1-59317-503-0
Retail $14.99

CD-ROM K20050CD
Retail $24.95

Real Community

Early Christians "had all things in common" and helped one another with all of life's needs. How can Christian teens do so today?

Book 978-1-59317-502-3
Retail $14.99

CD-ROM K10050CD
Retail $24.95

Christ the Re-Creator

We are told that our personality is set by the time we reach our teenage years. But what if God could reshape our attitudes and make us brand-new?

Book 978-1-59317-367-8
Retail $14.99

CD-ROM K10059CD
Retail $24.95

Fulfillment of the Ages

For thousands of years, God has promised his people a place of their own. Now he has fulfilled that promise in the church.

Book 978-1-59317-313-5
Retail $14.99

CD-ROM K30058CD
Retail $24.95

Know Your Patriarchs and Matriarchs

Can we learn anything useful from godly people of ancient times? This study of Old Testament heroes may surprise you.

Book 978-1-59317-304-3
Retail $14.99

CD-ROM K20051CD
Retail $24.95

The Doctor Is In

Christ offers his followers both spiritual and physical health. If our health fails, what does that say about our relationship with him?

Book 978-1-59317-308-1
Retail $14.99

CD-ROM K40051CD
Retail $24.95

Jesus Christ: Portrait of God

People disagree about who Jesus was—prophet, teacher, miracle worker, or holy man. What does the Bible tell us about him?

Book 978-1-59317-305-0
Retail $14.99

CD-ROM K40056CD
Retail $24.95

How It All Started

The debate over Creationism vs. evolution troubles many young believers. What does the Bible say about this, and what difference does it make in our daily lives?

Book 978-1-59317-558-0
Retail $14.99

CD-ROM K30051CD
Retail $24.95

The Work of Christ

Christ invites us to become his brothers and sisters in God's family. How is this different from the way God dealt with people in ancient times?

Book 978-1-59317-559-7
Retail $14.99

CD-ROM K10052CD
Retail $24.95

EVALUATION FORM

The Work of Christ

Community size: : _____ Church size: _____ Class size: _____

Average preparation time: _____ Class length: _____

My class is made up of:_____ Sixth graders   _____ Ninth graders

_____ Seventh graders   _____ Tenth graders

_____ Eighth graders   _____ Eleventh graders

_____ Twelfth graders

Please rate the following on a scale of *1* (never) to *10* (always):

- Were the instructions clear and user-friendly?   _____

- Was the content challenging enough for students?   _____

- Were the activities adequate for this age level?   _____

- Did you use the Portable Sanctuaries? (Y/N)   _____

- Did you use the Digital Bridges CD? (Y/N)   _____

Which sessions and areas worked best for you? _____

_____

Which sessions and areas should be changed or improved? _____

_____

Suggestions and Comments: _____

_____

_____

_____

Your full name: _____

Congregation Name, City, and State: _____

Phone number (_____)_____ E-mail _____

-----fold here-----

-----fold here-----

NAME________________________________
ADDRESS______________________________
CITY/STATE/ZIP_________________________
* Don't forget your return address! Postage is free!

NO POSTAGE
NECESSARY
IF MAILED
IN THE
UNITED STATES

BUSINESS REPLY MAIL
FIRST-CLASS MAIL PERMIT NO. 1233 ANDERSON IN

POSTAGE WILL BE PAID BY ADDRESSEE

JOSEPH D. ALLISON, PUBLISHER
CHURCH OF GOD MINISTRIES
PO BOX 2420
ANDERSON, IN 46018-2420